LAITHWAITE'S
GREAT WINE TREK

LAITHWAITE'S

GREAT WINE TREK

A journey through
every wine region of the world

TONY LAITHWAITE

FOREWORD BY HUGH JOHNSON

PART ONE

FRANCE

HARRAP

Perrier-Jouët

Designed and produced by Autumn Publishing Ltd,
10 Eastgate Square, Chichester.

First published in Great Britain in 1985 by Harrap Limited,
19-23 Ludgate Hill, London EC4M 7PD.

© 1985 Tony Laithwaite

Cover photographs John Sims, London
Photographs Tony Laithwaite
Additional photographs photo scope, France

Editor Alan Wakeford
Design Cecil Smith

ISBN 0 245-54310-4   (cased)
ISBN 0 245-54311-2   (paper)

Printed in Italy by Tipolitografia G Canale & C SpA
in association with Keats European Ltd.

Introduction

SINCE 1965 I've lived in a magic world. It has obsessed me, 24 hours a day for 20 years. (I mostly dream about wine!) Not just the wine itself but the people, places, history, traditions, food. I also love the 'trading' and building a business must be one of the most satisfying of human activities. And... I've always had this urge to tell everyone about this magic world. I thought it mean for wine merchants to indulge themselves in all the magic; the travels in beautiful sunny countries, the extravagant hospitality, the fascination of a craft industry — the only surviving craft industry of any size in the Western World — and then just fob off the customer with a bald wine list entry.

'Château Rahoul', 1979, Graves — fine, yes, but what about all the stories — the man who created the vineyard, who fought over it, won and lost it? What about the beauty of the place, the very special way those grapes are handled and their wine raised and nurtured with as much love and attention as given any child?

I've always thought the customer deserved as much of this as he wanted. I've tried to produce it in many ways. Hence 'Bordeaux Direct' and hence 'The Sunday Times Wine Club' which followed. And hence, now, this book.

Now, I don't think I can write. No false modesty here — I'm *sure* I can't. There are so many superb researchers and wordsmiths in the wine game. But I've been encouraged such a lot.

So I dedicate this book to the naggers.

To my mother who's always thought my every action was the greatest event in history and passed on to me her own 'affable fool' personality which seems to amuse. To HJ, unquestioned king of wine writers, who told me a good glass or two always helps the inspiration and get on with it, will you, lad. To the lady upon whose garden wall I once sat, diverting her from the weeding with sales patter and sample glasses, who remembered, and when her son grew up to be a publisher... To the book trade lady now in New York who promised she'd buy lots and lots if only...

And, of course, to Barbara, who now has to have treatment for the poor sore little arms that have been pushing her big lump of a husband along now for so many years.

Tony Laithwaite

7

Contents

Château Lonqueville, Médoc.

Foreword

TONY Laithwaite stumbled across the wine trade by happy accident. He was on an archaeological dig in the Dordogne from Durham University. He found lodgings with a kindly French couple who have a little vineyard. Monsieur ran the local, modestly prosperous, growers' cooperative. Tony started to help in the co-op, liked what he drank, and had the sense to see that people back in England would like it too.

He ran a little van to and fro, painted Bordeaux Direct on the sides, and rented a railway arch in Windsor, where on Saturday mornings a trickle of the curious soon turned into a stream of the grateful. Tony learned about wine the direct way, and learned to be direct about wine. When we first met he expected, I could see, a set of prejudices in favour

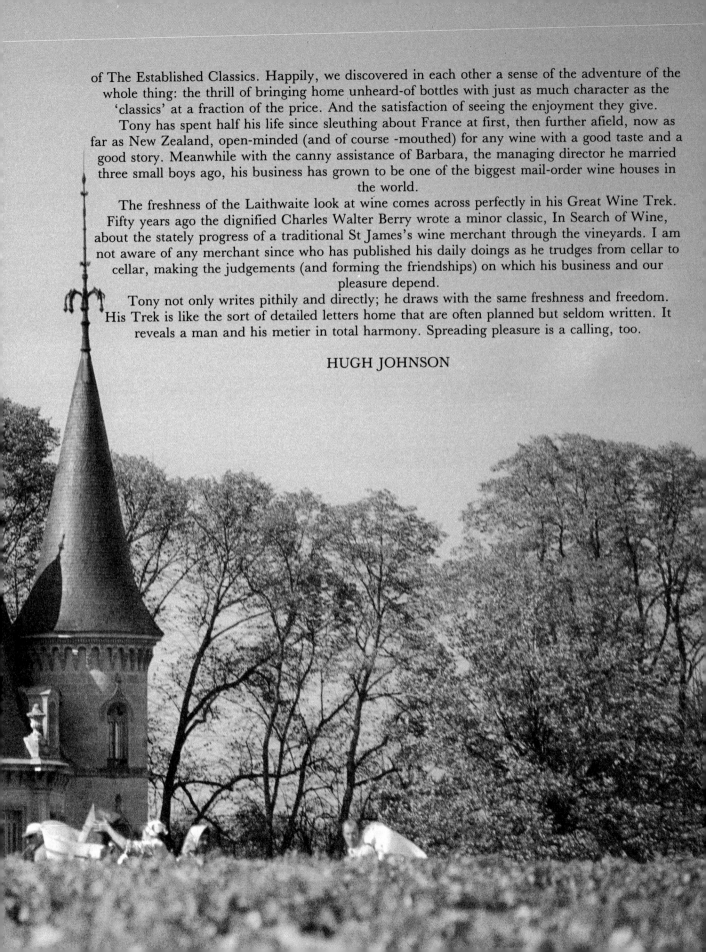

of The Established Classics. Happily, we discovered in each other a sense of the adventure of the whole thing: the thrill of bringing home unheard-of bottles with just as much character as the 'classics' at a fraction of the price. And the satisfaction of seeing the enjoyment they give.

Tony has spent half his life since sleuthing about France at first, then further afield, now as far as New Zealand, open-minded (and of course -mouthed) for any wine with a good taste and a good story. Meanwhile with the canny assistance of Barbara, the managing director he married three small boys ago, his business has grown to be one of the biggest mail-order wine houses in the world.

The freshness of the Laithwaite look at wine comes across perfectly in his Great Wine Trek. Fifty years ago the dignified Charles Walter Berry wrote a minor classic, In Search of Wine, about the stately progress of a traditional St James's wine merchant through the vineyards. I am not aware of any merchant since who has published his daily doings as he trudges from cellar to cellar, making the judgements (and forming the friendships) on which his business and our pleasure depend.

Tony not only writes pithily and directly; he draws with the same freshness and freedom. His Trek is like the sort of detailed letters home that are often planned but seldom written. It reveals a man and his metier in total harmony. Spreading pleasure is a calling, too.

HUGH JOHNSON

—STAGE 1—
Up the Dordogne

THE storm had cut a swathe right down my intended route. The evening before I had stood in the dark in our vineyard at La Clarière and watched brilliant flashes lighting up the eastern sky, like a battle. It was a storm that made headline news in France. On television I saw an *expert-météo* explain with an airy wave that this sort of stuff usually went straight to *Les Anglais*! But this was a rogue depression which had swerved into France — Madame Thatcher's doing, for sure! In the morning as I swerved to avoid the splintered tree trunks that had not yet been chainsawed, I did wonder if someone up there was passing a warning about this Great Wine Trek folly. But, on a Monday in November, the downpour ceased as dawn broke, and I set off from our French *domaine* down through Castillon-la-Bataille and across the little River Lidoire into the *département* of the Dordogne.

There is no dramatic change of scenery from Gironde to Dordogne. As at La Clarière the vineyards are mixed in with maize, pasture and woodland. Not like the monoculture of St-Emilion, just a bit to the west. But as I drove further east up the Dordogne valley the names began to change and the northern and southern slopes no longer carried the grand name of Bordeaux. Instead I passed Montravel, Rosette and Pécharmant on the north bank; Saussignac and Monbazillac on the south; good old Bergerac

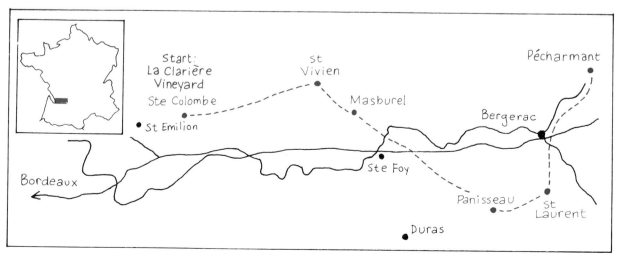

The starting point of the Great Trek, Ste-Colombe, near Bordeaux, where we have our own vineyard.

both sides and Côtes de Duras a bit further to the south in the *département* of Lot et Garonne—all *appellation contrôlée*.

My first appointment was 8.30am (can't hang about in our business, early bird, worms and all that—the *métier* of trendy-drive-over-and-fetch-it-young-British-wine-merchants is a touch over-crowded these days!). Château de Masburel was an appropriate start to this mammoth venture. A huge log fire blazed in the huge kitchen fireplace; copper pans sparkled and breakfast was hurriedly cleared. The owner, however, was not your usual Dordogne farmer but a retired chemist from Marseilles who had come in from the heat and noise to help his son make wine in the cool green of the Perigord. I did the obligatory cellar tour, admired an unusually polished and white-washed cellar and enjoyed the slightly amateur bursting enthusiasms of the new wine grower; I have the same naive trait myself. We sat at the kitchen

Just to keep busy, a number of Dordogne wine-growers also grow tobacco.

table, and discussed prices—all rather rapidly. They were high-ish, but the 'half-sweet' Haut Montravel looked a fair bet; it had a lovely fruit aroma and was clean without the low acid tackiness you often get in these whites, a factor which has lost them a lot of popularity in the face of other medium whites from, say, Anjou or Germany. We rushed goodbyes; *filer à l'Anglais* (to rush like the English) is a common French expression highlighting a national trait which most of us, I suppose, would imagine we had lost—certainly when compared with the average French motorist. But what they really mean is that the English just like to say goodbye and push off. For the French, goodbyes, to be correct, must be long and lingering. I *file* to the cooperative winery in the village of St-Vivien. Here I found quite a difference. Cooperative wineries really are sensationally ugly. In the inter-war period when most of them were built they really worked at the ugliness. At St-Vivien, not content with sticking a vast pile of concrete in the middle of a pretty stone-walled, Roman-tiled, cute village, they piled a reinforced concrete crenellated tower on top; a similar disfigurement occurs down the road at Montcaret. Is this perhaps a defence system against rapacious Bordeaux wine merchants? But I must not go on so. The head of the Dordogne Cooperative Union has threatened to kill me if I continue to be rude about his precious *caves*. Of course, I love them really. They work without artifice, guile or pretence to make good wine less expensively than independent vineyards.

Coopérative de St-Vivien
St-Vivien, 24830 Velines

So we moved in on St-Vivien's cooperative and Foucaud was there, having arrived a little earlier in his flashy GX. The golden boy of the cooperative wine-makers now has vast influence. He actually decides what most of Bordeaux will taste like, such is the enormous power of the Cooperative Union. We sip some brand new

Montravel which is a fresh grape-like juice, although afterwards the mouth feels like it has just drunk a very dry wine.

It will make a good aperitif but was a trifle young when we drank it; we much preferred an earlier Montravel. A word of advice for those who plan to visit the area: you will probably prefer to pass up the pretty farmhouse in favour of a much keener price from the cooperative. Try this Montravel as an aperitif with rich fish dishes, or just sip a glass while you watch television. Serve it viciously cold.

I then moved on to the 1982 Duras Sauvignon which Foucaud had brought along. It is a lovely wine made for the first time ever from maximum-ripe grapes. They usually prefer a little immaturity to provide the green 'zip' in the wine, but in this particular year everything was brought on much faster by some boiling hot days in September. In just three days the harvest was super ripe, healthy and ready for picking (they had to pick fast). I think the wine will appeal to the British who are generally less keen on acidity than the French, and for my part, I think the wine is genuinely better with the greenness. Duras Sauvignon is best bottled and drunk as soon as it stops fizzing or preferably fractionally before it stops.

Cave de Duras (Berticot)
47120 Duras

They have only been making the pure Merlot for three years at Duras. Previously, as with claret, the Merlot was blended with the tougher, more aromatic Cabernets. But Merlot made by *macération carbonique*—that frightening-sounding fermentation method—really does flow down the gullet without touching the edges! It is a genuine low-tannin alternative to the omnipresent 'Beauj'.

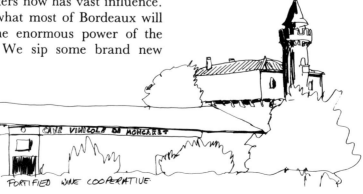

FORTIFIED WINE COOPERATIVE.

Woods, vines and pastures in the Dordogne.

Top wine-making professionals really are a race apart! We had finished, Foucaud was just off to another cellar at St-Vincent de Pertignas to pick the best vats of claret with Professor Peynaud, the daddy of all tasters. At that moment the sales manager of the cooperatives arrived; the two were all of 20 yards apart when instead of a 'Bonjour' or similar salutation, we heard, 'My God, Puel … the petrol!' Without a mention of nice weather or anything visual, it was a case of nose first every time, and sure enough, when he checked, Robert Puel found a fractionally-leaking jerry-can in his car boot! The fumes had slightly impregnated his clothes and had we arrived earlier, we would have ruined the tasting; we moved on.

The rolling Dordogne countryside looked freshly washed. Visibility was exceptionally good and the November sunshine made everything sparkle. Nature was really rather overdoing the colour scheme: trees of gold, light green pasture, dark green pine, khaki oaks, tall brilliant yellow poplars, golden vines, red vines, brown leaves on the ground and EEC-glut sized mounds of Golden Delicious beneath their bare, black trees. The Dordogne châteaux began at Gageac which is a gem of the 15th century. It stands tall and dignified, all turrets and towers and steep-roofed in grey licheny stone. As I got lost and more lost, I went down narrower and narrower roads and kept discovering more and more hidden medieval glories.

A lady in a floral pinny, carrying a bucket of milk, finally directed me to Panisseau. Panisseau is a 'mini' château. It is Emile Becker's great love, and as if to prove it he makes wine—very success-fully—just to pay for the restoration costs. He lives

The Château de Panisseau.

on the top floor, his sister on the first and occasionally visitors are allowed in to inspect the ground floor. Imagine scraping the plaster off your living room walls and finding four-hundred-year-old panelling! Emile did, and that was the start of his obsession. The clay tiles on the floor bear the paw marks of a naughty dog, dead these four hundred years.

The aroma of the new white wine burst from the sample bottle. The wine stuns the palate on impact but is hollow thereafter which is why Monsieur Becker always blends the new with 50 per cent or so of the old, making a mellow wine, long flavoured and full. Blending vintages is still an amazingly rare thing—folk so love a number. But it has worked well for Panisseau. Be warned that Emile Becker likes his privacy and his Alsatian likes a bit of leg. I always take a companion or two to Panisseau (sorry about the leg, Charles). I adjourned to Bergerac for lunch at the Hôtel de Bordeaux. They have the excellent idea of a 'local' menu which came at the modest price of 70 francs or so and included three local wines selected to fit the courses.

Bergerac - riverfront.

Monsieur Becker
Château de Panisseau
Thénac, 24240 Sigoulès

In the post-lunch haze I moved on up river to find Pécharmant, which proved less easy. Pécharmant is a wine area that almost disappeared but which is gradually making a come-back. I discovered a very big, dark wine—similar to a sort of 'super' Bergerac—made by only about six growers. The cooperatives made a Pécharmant that I have bought in the past, but theirs is usually light and hard to tell from Bergerac. This time having tried three (pretty comprehensive—50 per cent of the crop) I plumped for Maurice Girardet. He is another new wine-maker and, it transpired, an ex-headmaster who blesses the day the death of his brother-in-law released him from timetabling and the PTA.

He has introduced considerable innovation in his two short years: first, the rotating vats which are like giant cement mixers and extract a better colour and flavour from grapeskins, and second, the new gentle wine presses. The Malbec grape Clos Peyrelevade is very good value and exceptionally full and dark. It is on the scale, if not quite in the sophisticated style, of a top class claret.

Monsieur Maurice Girardet
Clos Peyrelevade
Pécharmant, 24100 Bergerac

Then I tried the good old Bergerac, visiting the cooperative cellars at St-Laurent to look at vat samples. I talked to head oeneologist Paul Gagnard who extends a long-standing loyalty to me when it comes to choosing the best vats. The loyalty stems back to the golden days of 1968 when he used to play hooker to my wing forward in the Castillon-la-Bataille XV. He never lets his old team mate down and proved as much this visit.

Panisseau

Cave St-Laurent des Vignes (Unidor)
24240 Sigoulès

—STAGE 2—
The Causses

MONBAZILLAC is a small village, a large château and a wine region 'on its way up', a few minutes south of Bergerac. The vineyards slope down to the north which is unusual, but similar to the best Sauternes vineyards. The happy result of this feature is that the shade encourages the growth of an obliging little mould called *Botrytis Cinerea* or *Pourriture Noble* (Noble Rot!). The *Botrytis* feeds on the water of the grape rather than the sugar, thus enhancing the richness of the grape and allowing the production of a rich dessert wine. Château Pion is one of a quintet of properties belonging to the cooperative of Monbazillac. These fine Monbazillacs have a rich almond flavour and a sweetness that is well balanced by acidity and bitterness to avoid any cloying. They are, thanks to their clean finish, just as good an 'aperitif' as 'digestif'. Not a lot of people know this. Why? Sweetness is 'registered' by the tip of the tongue and therefore first, which means that this is, all most people notice in a Monbazillac. Bitterness and acidity are 'registered' further back at the sides…too late! Try concentrating for longer next time, if you pick up the secondary flavours you will see why Monbazillac does, in fact, tend to improve appetite rather than deaden it. Serve nice and cold.

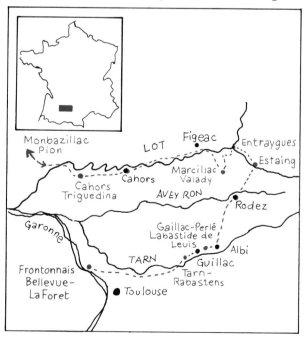

Château Pion (Unidor)
Monbazillac, 24240 Sigoulès

I moved on towards the Lot valley and Cahors. At Puy l'Evêque I arrived very late to a grumpy reception at the hotel. Soon, however, the mean old devil scowled off and two pretty barmaids provided an *Assiette Anglaise* of cold meats of a generosity never likely to be found in old Angleterre. I woke to spectacular views of the valley of the Lot. The countryside of the lower valley, between the river's extravagant meander-

Lunch break at a Cahors vineyard.

ings, was spread like a map below my eyrie so it was easy to spot my first vineyard. In 1976, I had picked out Clos Triguedina as a likely supplier because they seemed to win a lot of medals. But one thing or another kept me away until today. Monsieur Baldès is a remarkable man consumed passionately by his work. He has the most advanced wine cellars I have ever seen and no expense is spared to make the best wines it is possible to make.

A little history: Cahors was a major commercial trading centre in the Middle Ages when bankers from Lombardy settled there. The valley was similarly rich and highly developed agriculturally with fertile lower pastures, sheep-grazed barren *causses* above and vines hung down the steep valley sides. The vines produced the red wine that was prized above all others in England—no local chauvinism, that, I checked it up myself. 'Black' Cahors used to travel down river (first the Lot and then the Garonne) to Bordeaux and on to England. But the later growth of the wine industry in Bordeaux itself, along with the phylloxera vine louse, decimated the Cahors vineyards. Only three or four growers persisted stubbornly after the louse finished its work and among them was the grandfather of Monsieur Baldès. The steep slopes were abandoned altogether and ruined growers planted hybrid vines that pumped out lots of 'plonk' nothing at all like the old Cahors. Fortunately for them, the Baldès family vineyards lay, if not on the steep

scree slopes, then second best, on the shallow slopes of a big gravel bed. They replanted the traditional Auxerrois vine, at 70 per cent the main constituent of true Cahors, plus a little Merlot from Bordeaux and the tiny bitter black Tannat grape that enables their wine to last forever. There were countless legal battles to re-establish the traditions, the granting of VDQS (2nd division) status, then at last, full *appellation contrôlée* in 1971. I got all this and much more from Monsieur Baldès in his *caveau personnel*. Believe me, he is no mean talker!

We finished up on a 1943 Triguedina from an old opaque bottle—war-time issue?—that was still vibrant and alive and proved the incredible longevity of this wine. But the 1980 Clos Triguedina is a lovely wine with an aroma which is uniquely Cahors. It is uncannily reminiscent of the smell of a fresh packet of tea. What kind of tea? Let's not get too carried away, say Ceylon. The wine is heavy, full and dark yet already smooth. It costs the same as good Bordeaux but it is well worth it. I left Triguedina with every intention of returning frequently.

Monsieur Baldès et Fils
Clos Triguedina
Puy l'Evêque 46700

The Lot valley beyond Cahors becomes a large sheer-sided gulley, steadily growing steeper with more waterfalls. The vines die away again only to reappear unexpectedly in steep small patches around Decazville and Roque-Bouillac. They are vertical vineyards—similar to the old Cahors vineyards perhaps? I left the river via the lunar landscape of the zinc mines at Viviez which reminded me of England's industrial north; and the similarity is reinforced by a countryside of rolling moors, chunky stone houses in red sandstone like Pennine villages, and an odd, wine-coloured soil. Marcillac is one of the rarities I was looking for up here in the Aveyron, which in spite of its VDQS appellation I was not sure still existed. But at Valady, a neighbouring village to Marcillac I found a little wine cooperative. The director, a Monsieur Metje made me warmly welcome. 'Marcillac wine to Britain? Quelle idée!' I tried a sample and found it like Beaujolais in style though less so in taste—more like blackcurrants and raspberries with a touch of pepper. It is made from the local Fer Servadou or Mansois grape which is a distant relative of the Cabernets. All in all it is a highly original yet inexpensive wine. We learned that a hundred years ago they made 10 million litres but now only 2 to 3 million litres! It was never an export wine like Cahors but more of a local wine. However, phylloxera and the new railway which brought in cheap Midi wines combined to kill it. Although, since 1965 it has been making something of a come-back, thanks mainly to the fact that traditionally most Parisian bistros are run by *auvergnats* from this area. These *'bougnats'* as they are called occasionally like to serve their home wine. Monsieur Metje also gave me the good news that two further wine regions were still alive and hidden in valleys to the north-east.

Cave de Valady
Valady, 12330 Marcillac Vallon

I trailed off down narrow lanes past the Abbey of Conques. There are steep vineyards everywhere but where does all the wine go? At one point I emerged on to the top of a sort of vast moor and the high hills of Cantal lay in the far distance before me. It was as though I was on the roof of France. Then after a couple of sharp turns I stopped to admire the staggering view. Like a wine merchant's little El Dorado, there in a crevasse-like wooded valley where two rivers joined (the Lot and the Truyère), the town of Entraygues nestled around its château; steep, terraced vineyards such

as are virtually never seen in France these days completed the picture. I wound downwards to the town in haste and looked for my quarry. Monsieur Viguier turned out to be startlingly young (19), having been catapulted from agricultural college to running the farm by his father's ill-health. He was pottering in one of the most ancient,

The Author in early morning negotiations.

cobwebby, dusty, old cellars I have ever seen. He farms four hectares which is more than half the current Entraygues et du Fel VDQS area (although in 1860 the area covered over a thousand hectares).

With the help of the granitic soil of the Entraygues, Jean-Marc Viguier makes, for the most part, a full, round dry white from a local version of the Chenin Blanc grape. Fel which is the next village along makes a red on schist-type soils. The Viguier label shows the vineyards more than a little idealized, more, perhaps, as they were a hundred years ago. Entraygues would be enjoyable for a holiday: with its woods, fishing, a nice looking hotel, good food and above all a wine which is (a) nice, (b) rare and (c) inexpensive, it would be hard to go wrong. In addition there is a little railcar track up the Dordogne from Bordeaux that stops everywhere including Castillon-la-Bataille (my home town in France) and finally ends at Aurillac just ten miles away from here. How about a litle old-fashioned train travel next summer? I fell for Entraygues! I left Jean-Marc a touch bemused—he had never met any kind of wine merchant and had never sold so much wine in one day.

Jean-Marc Viguier
Les Buis, 12140 Entraygues

Labastide de Lévis boasts the biggest winery in France, a cooperative, of course, which sits on a hill. Inside, like the boiler room of the QE2 are machines to crush, press, centrifuge, concentrate, chill, heat, fizz and bottle. I have been there on a harvest evening when at least a mile of tractors still queued to disgorge their grapes. Their greatest creation at Labastide is the Perlé, a wine with a few residual CO_2 bubbles left in after fermentation to give it extra 'zip' and freshness. Gaillac makes wines of all colours as well as fruit juice and real fizz, but you should just concentrate on the Perlé—and tell friends it is a Mâcon! What's a little fib between friends?

Cave Coopérative des Coteaux de Gaillac et du Pays Cordais
81150 Labastide de Lévis (Tarn)

This region also makes a Vin du Pays—the Côtes du Tarn. It is widely seen in Britain now which is not surprising as it is France's cheapest wine. If that does not sound too 'tasty' (though it can be), try the red we get from the 'other' cooperative group in the region of Rabastens. (The two cooperatives hate each other, which helps keep prices down.)

Cave de Rabastens
33 Route d'Albe, 81800 Rabastens (Tarn)

Have you ever heard of the Côtes du Frontonnais? It is an AOC and the wine of Toulouse. This is another region very much on the up again, having been around since the 12th century at least. They make white and pink but the interesting thing is a red made of the unique Negrette grape grown on deep Médoc-like gravel beds. Château Bellevue La Forêt, a very modern looking, impeccably run outfit, also grows Cabernet (from Bordeaux), Gamay (from Beaujolais), and Syrah (from Hermitage). This is quite an original mix and one that has won so many medals that it must be the best of the dozen or so producers in the area. It is definitely worth a try as an excellent 'claret-substitute-with-a-difference'.

Monsieur Hector de Galand
Château Bellevue La Forêt
31620 Fronton

The Viguier Cellar - Entraygues

—STAGE 3—
The Languedoc Hills

It may seem strange but I am always fascinated by the way the green woods and pasture of central France become the arid scrub of the Languedoc (the Midi) in a matter of a mile or two of going over the Montagne Noire. It must be useful to live on such a border: when the rain gets you down you can just pop over the other side for a sunbathe; or if you are dehydrating in those rocky vineyards it is easy just to nip north for a quick paddle in a cool trout stream!

Early on Armistice Day I had left a grey, damp Castres full of leering war veterans watching drum majorettes going through their paces. The green countryside was positively English. I drove east. To the south a looming dark mass topped with raincloud came closer: it was the Montagne Noire. It must be the dense covering of chestnut, oak and pine that earned it the appropriate name—black mountain. Just after Ferrals—with its field-walls of upright stone slabs similar to the ones around Hawkshead in the English lakes—the big change occurs. The clouds are left behind and behold the sun and the vista! Ahead were the Minervois, the valley of the Aude, Corbières and Roussillon; on the left I saw the Mediterranean and in the far distance Mont Canigou and the Pyrénées beckoned. I was already in the 'High Minervois' —all stones, scrub and abandoned vineyards. Up here any kind of cultivation is difficult. When I pulled off the road the scent of wild garlic grew strong where the tyres had crushed the little plants.

La Livinière was the first village I came to. I swept through past a byzantine-looking tower, white walls and lots of Midi gents in their Sunday best who greeted me with puzzled looks; G.B. plates are an oddity here in November. (The rude French say G.B. stands for *gueule de bois*, literally wooden-mouth or one who has drunk too much! Did you know?) I went to the cooperative to meet

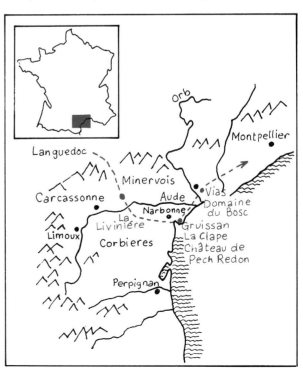

Monsieur Pisini in his barrel-ageing cellar.

ultra-modern winery alongside the old. He hires experts to classify only about a third of the old vineyard sites as acceptable to his new winery (and even if vineyards are accepted the growers are restricted to planting only the best vines). Finally he sits judge-like by the cellar entrance throughout the harvest, passing their grapes only if healthy and in good nick. Only *then* does he let their grapes in to be vinified, by himself alone, using the *macération carbonique* method. As a final touch he sends them to age in a barrel cellar (the barrels are second-hand from Chasse-Spleen), which is a unique luxury in the Midi where virtually everything is aged, if at all, in concrete vats.

Not surprisingly the wines sell for more than most Midi wines—but not a lot more. This is good for us, but means the Pisini-La-Livinière experiment is far from being called a success in the village. Poor Pisini is none too popular. On the other hand they said Marconi was daft too, and somebody has got to start improving the great mass of Midi wine before the lake bursts its banks. So, although for our sake and your sakes I would like to see the price kept down, I would also like to see the brave Pisini get more for his labours. Perhaps everyone should just buy more? Then we would all be happy!

Cave des Coteaux du Minervois
La Livinière
34210 Dionbac

I met Jean Demolombe at La Livinière; he has been 'my man in the Midi' since 1972. The bulk-wine-merchant business of this larger than life wine fanatic had just gone bankrupt when I visited him (tough times in France). However, he still has his own farm at Pech Redon and will 'broke' (an unfortunate term in the circumstances) other wine. I like to think I am a good wine finder, but in the Midi (the world's largest vineyard which is geologically as complex as could be and largely unmapped) I could not even start without the guidance of 'Jeanno'. We went up to Pech Redon, which is a sort of Wuthering Heights or Cold Comfort Farm, isolated in its own valley on top of that odd (and even more oddly named) little bit of hill between Narbonne and the sea called La Clape.

Le Coffre is a vast, square, stone block and a bit like that hill in 'Close Encounters'. It is the

the remarkable Monsieur Pisini, the cooperative President who claims to have a dirty *'sale'* character. He seemed totally charming to me but he must certainly have a strong will for he has bullied his cooperative members into a venture no other cooperative in the Midi has attempted. He has effectively created a cooperative within a cooperative to cream off the best wines of the village. Remember that Midi wine-growers are traditionally either curmudgeonly (they hate change and feel that the rest of wine-growing France has conspired to place them in their relatively impoverished state) or violent (they burn foreign wine lorries, smash the cellars of merchants suspected of importing Italian wine, proclaim they want 'Occitan' to be 'Libre' and remove sign posts to confound the poor tourist). Mostly they are the very old and stubborn former type, otherwise they are the younger, bearded, angry and extremist type.

So along comes this Pisini, who even sounds like an Italian, armed with EEC money to build an

The town of Minerve.

high point of La Clape and in its shadow lies the haunted-looking Château of Pech Redon. Jean has ignored the château and poured his money into replanting the vineyards to make a red that gets better every year. Since 1981, when the Cabernet Sauvignon grape was first incorporated in the blend, the red, in particular, has made big leaps forward.

Monsieur Jean Demolombe
Château de Pech Redon
La Clape, 11100 Narbonne

---

huge, soaring, racketing cloud of migrating starlings. Jean is gradually turning some of the outhouses into holiday homes. So much peace and space, so close to the Mediterranean in France must be unique. It is high up, so there is a long walk, or drive (in a solid car) to the beach, but there are no buildings or metalled roads down to the water just shrubs, aromatic pines and vineyards. La Clape is now a *site classé* (National Trust sort of thing), so luckily it is going to stay unspoilt. We went on up the coast to near Agde which is a nudist town. As it was November and bitterly cold we understood why they seemed to be staying in that day!

Pierre Bésinet is yet another fanatic—where do I get them all from? He is the one with vineyards

Pech Redon.

Soon there will be a Chardonnay white to add to his range which he says—and I agree—will really 'slay 'em'. My two trainees who were on the trek with me that day were each given a bottle on a long piece of string and instructed to fetch the new rosé from the vat as an accompaniment for the fresh grilled prawns just in from Port Gruissan. Ultra fresh wine for ultra fresh fish. And herb-baked lamb followed. All you have to do here for bouquet garni is go outside and grab a bit of whatever is not a vine. Wild thyme, rosemary, garlic, genever, mint, bay, fennel and a few others grow everywhere as weeds.

In the morning I woke before dawn to catch a spectacular sunrise over Le Coffre, animated by a

planted on a volcano—an extinct one mind you, he is not *that* eccentric. Domaine du Bosc is a huge rambling château situated on a *bosky* (a little hill with a wooded top). These hills are made of black cinders and the soil, which is positively lunar, supports nothing unless it is constantly watered. Given water, vines flourish and produce amazing results. Vines do best on well drained soil and this is the ultimate in good drainage. Bésinet has a number of different vine varieties, some of which are over thirty years old. Three, in particular, interested us: the astonishing Grenache that makes a super-pungent dry white; some Merlot that makes a sort of cinnamony, feather-soft, delightful red; and an ultra-smooth, extremely

gulpable, whole grape vinification blend of Cinsault and Syrah grape.

Monsieur Bésinet
Domaine du Bosc, 34450 Vias

The château, to be frank, was a tip, with irrigation pipes lying around beside other assorted rusty machinery. To be fair, a storm the night before had demolished a few trees and tipped a wine press into a ditch, which did not help; but it did seem that all that Bésinet really cared about was inside the vats! In a little courtyard there were six big steel cylinders. A little tap gushed into a glass and, whammy, this fresh wine shock-wave hit us ... all of five feet away. This is a pungent wine which stuns without warning. But, of course, as Monsieur Bésinet pointed out, if we had been able to smell any wine in his cellar, prior to opening the tap, he would have been most unhappy, because any wine aroma in the cellar is aroma lost to the wine. (Note for the future: avoid aromatic wine cellars.) Pierre ferments his whites at 14-18 degrees centigrade which is positively cold (I panic if my reds go below 30 degrees centigrade!) —it also takes weeks. And when it stops, or even a little before it stops (in order to retain some nice bubbles in the wine) he bottles—immediately. All the carefully tended flavour is locked up in a bottle

as soon as possible. It was only November when we visited, but some of Bésinet's new red as well as the white was already bottled. I mentioned he was an eccentric ... actually he is a genius.

The great advantage of Vin de Pays status is the lack of rules. The enterprising wine maker can experiment, bring in new vine varieties and bottle more or less what he likes. With AOC or VDQS status he is restricted to traditional vine varieties and methods. This is fine in Bordeaux but in the Hérault the traditions are—well largely—rubbish. The problem with this is how does the PBC (poor bloody consumer) tell from the label if his Vin de Pays is from a go-go clever grower, or if it is just the bog-standard, bottom-of-the-range from the local merchant or cooperative. He cannot—but *you* can (by listening to me)!

Later, we were sitting on top of a Midi hill. It was very cold, but we were admiring the view while munching saucisson and cheese and swigging from the bottle (a habit I detest, but there was no alternative). This was a snatched farewell lunch with Jean. I had taken a good look at the north part of the Midi and made all the visits mentioned—not bad for a 36 hour stay. Such is life—I had really intended this Great Wine Trek to be a chance to retrace my wine trips of the last 15 years at a leisurely pace. Fat chance of that, and I doubt that I will even get any sympathy!

—STAGE 4—
East Bank of the Rhône

I was on my way to the Wine Fair of Orange held every January as the first great *concours* (wine competition) of the year. I had dreamed of going for many years and longed to escape Britain at dead of winter for a first snatch of sun. And sunny it was this year, quite warm too. In the sheltered yard in front of the Provençal village

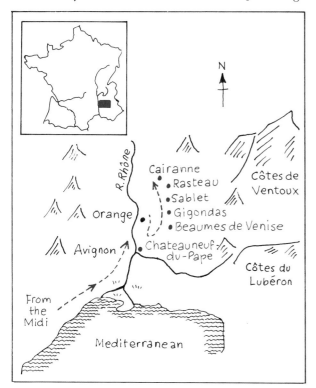

house we had been loaned, I could sit on a step in the sun and watch small Number One son get delirious and drenched in the village fountain. No sign of pneumonia and only January 28th! I turned up at 8.00am for the *concours*; I was the first of something like three hundred and fifty judges, who were divided five to a table. With seventy plus tables, each with about twenty wines, there was a lot of tasting! Away on the count of 10.00am... give or take half an hour or so. *Déliberation des Jurys*: rinse, swill, sip, gurgle, 'hmm', splatt—not a pretty sight!

I was judging Côtes du Ventoux Reds and Lubéron Whites and Rosés. And although they spelled my name Greek (Laithxwaite) they made me president of my table. It was a singular honour and somewhat worrying because I had to give guidance; I mean on what scale do you judge? Giving preferences is fairly easy but scoring is relative to what criteria? We lashed out. To our top white and top red, my panel awarded gold medals, with silvers for the seconds (the rosés were appalling: zero). When the results were being read out later I got a bit nervous as many juries failed to award any golds; but then our top white went on to be judged 'Wine of the Show' by the 'Super-Jury', so I felt we had been fair. I found out afterwards (all the tasting is done 'blind', of course), that the little cooperative group at Tour d'Aigues were in

Looking north up the east bank of the Rhône.

the medals so I ordered their Lubéron white at fantastic value. Another medal winner was 'Pascal' otherwise known as Denis Cheron. He makes a lovely soft little Ventoux from grapes he buys (unusual in France) from those attractive vineyards that cascade down the slopes of the huge Ventoux mountain.

Domaine Jean Pascal et Fils
Gigondas, 84190 Beaumes-de-Venise

Cellier de Marrenon
84240 La Tour d'Aigues

The problem of how to cover the rest of the great variety of the Rhône on this trek was solved by deciding just to go up the east bank this time and leave the west for later. I set off on Monday, much encouraged by the fact that my southern suppliers that day had won between them four golds and six silvers. To Châteauneuf. Châteauneuf-du-Pape is one of those super evocative wine names like Chablis or Nuits-Saint-Georges, uttered with reverence by the older wine drinker, usually as part of the phrase 'whatever happened to the good old ... I used to get for three bob down at the off-licence'. It never existed, that is what happened! As writer after writer has explained, before the French *appellation contrôlée* rules were enforced over here, in 1972 or thereabouts, Châteauneuf was really no more than a brand name for any red wine from anywhere! The real

thing, grown within the village boundaries has always been expensive, mainly because it is usually good and partly because the concept of *appellation contrôlée* was invented here. A certain Baron le Roy dreamed up the scheme because he disliked seeing his village name being stuck on bottles of red North African paint-stripper. My first call—Château de Beaucastel.

Below what appears to be a simple farmhouse are an astonishing number of bottles: caverns full, row upon row. François Perrin makes wine 'built-

to-last'. It is old-style Châteauneuf and there is no question that Beaucastel is a BIG WINE! It needs ten years at least, says François, and looking at his stocks he intends to try and enforce that delay. I bought some more of the 1979 I had acquired last time. 'It tastes of leather and makes me think of

Growing vines in cobblestones is an unusual feature of wine-growing in the Rhône Valley.

Château du Trignon

liquorice' I wrote, which certainly will not sell it. It is so dark that it hints at a Barolo—you can't see daylight through the younger vintages! It also has considerable acid, tannin and alcohol, and makes me think of a medieval wine. It evokes huge fires, haunches of venison on pewter platters, hairy horsemen in big riding boots, jesters, Robin Hood brought in in chains! Remember the film? It is wine that went out when the more perfumy, gentle, Beau Brummel type claret and burgundy came in.

François Perrin
Château de Beaucastel
84350 Courthézon

Vaccarese! Counoise! Terret Noir! Bourboulenc! Roussanne!—with wild-sounding grapes like that mixed in with the usual Grenache, Mourvèdre, Syrah and so on, how could anyone make delicate wine? Perrin does not attempt to, he waits for time to tame the brute. Without filtering, the brown sediment encrusts the green glass of that heavy arms-emblazoned Châteauneuf bottle. Lily-livered Beaujolais bibbers beware: this wine bites! The very rare white Châteauneuf made at Beaucastel is by no means as tough. It is made from the Roussanne grape which is just about the same as the Marsanne of Hermitage; nonetheless it is still a somewhat chunky wine and not for the delicate.

To Trignon. I arrived late at Trignon—a simple farmhouse, with a fountain, it is one of Provence's prettiest hill-villages. André and Colette Roux must be my dearest friends in the wine business. I meet hundreds of marvellous people, and lots of extravagant personalities (it is the wine that does it), but coming to Trignon feels like coming home. Does this sort of friendship influence my choice of wine? Of course it does! I would do anything to sell André's wine. And why not? I first tasted it back in 1971, and it has been good, nay brilliant, ever since. I would say, without doubt that he rates as one of the top five wine-makers of the Rhône valley. He specializes in *macération carbonique* (terrible name, so we coined the phrase 'whole grape vinification') which means that he ferments uncrushed grapes in an oxygen-free atmosphere.

André Roux
Château du Trignon
Gigondas, 84190 Beaumes-de-Venise

We ambled down the steps, then along the

Early spring in Sablet.

tunnel to the cellars, to taste a dry white that is a wine making *tour de force* in this hot country. It was even more so ten years ago when no-one else knew how he did it. How he prevented all those lovely fruit aromas from boiling away no-one could understand. Now there are many other good white wine makers in the south, but André still leads. Then we climbed ducking among the rafters to dip our glasses deep into the purple pools below the trapdoors on the deep vats of ten thousand litres or so of wildly aromatic—even when near freezing cold—Rhône 'Villages' wines. André has vineyards in the villages of Sablet, in Rasteau to the north and Gigondas to the south. His Sablet is 50 per cent Grenache and 50 per cent Syrah grape; a dark purple thing hinting at bilberries and cassis when young but maturing remarkably fast to acquire in addition a complex secondary bouquet of 'woodland floor'. Just think of a damp, late autumn morning walk in the woods ... kicking the leaves ... mushrooms ... mildew ... warm, slightly-dubious, live earth, and you will have it.

His Rasteau is 50 per cent Grenache, 50 per cent Mourvèdre (the rustic Bandol grape) adding, it seems to me, even more interest than the Syrah gives to the Sablet. The pure Mourvèdre wine is so rough and tough it is like trying to drink scaffold board, but blended, it provides a sumptuous 'Basso Profundo' bass-line to the Grenache treble. I think it is André Roux's finest wine. However, that honour goes in most people's view to his Gigondas. Gigondas, of course, stands alone; like Châteauneuf it disdains the necessity of adding 'Rhône' to its name. Gigondas wines are easily the equal of Châteauneufs, but they are less well known, and therefore cheaper ... just!

I continued on my way to see a man who can equal and possibly exceed the number of medals won in wine *concours* by our André. Abel Rabasse-Charavin is more the classic, more the horny-handed son of the soil than bookish André. He is adamant that he owes it all to being blessed with the most perfect south-facing slope in all the southern Rhône—he is modest in every way. Discreet little signs point the way up to his house,

André Roux.

Gigondas.

Sorting grapes at Château du Trignon.

in contrast to some of his neighbours and relatives who like to see their names painted in red six feet tall along the stone walls. He or his bubbly, chatty wife will take you to the tasting room (actually a very cluttered cellar) to sip this and that. The thing to watch for is the Cairanne, Côtes du Rhône 1981. It is a fantastic winner of four gold medals: Orange, Paris, Mâcon and Bordeaux—the 'Grand Slam'. He said it was his best since 1976 and furthermore that it was a backward child only coming good in February 1982. There has been no sign of retardation ·since, believe me, from this classic Côtes du Rhône. Abel finished off the session with his Vin Doux Naturel. He had vines in next-door Rasteau, and like André Roux enjoys making a little AOC Rasteau sweet dessert wine for fun.

Abel Rabasse-Charavin
Les Coteaux St. Martin, 84290 Cairanne

But for this journey I really had to go and buy the much more famous AOC Beaumes-de-Venise, made not from Grenache but with the grapiest of all grapes: the Muscat. The village cooperative cellar of Beaumes put theirs in what looked like perfume bottles; but forget the bottle, the wine is superb, if not unique. You can keep it in the fridge; it lasts as long as you can resist it, and one tiny chilled thimbleful rescues even the dullest of desserts or the tiredest of cooks.

Cave des Vignerons de Beaumes-de-Venise
84190 Beaumes-de-Venise (Vaucluse)

—STAGE 5—
Further up the
East Bank of the Rhône

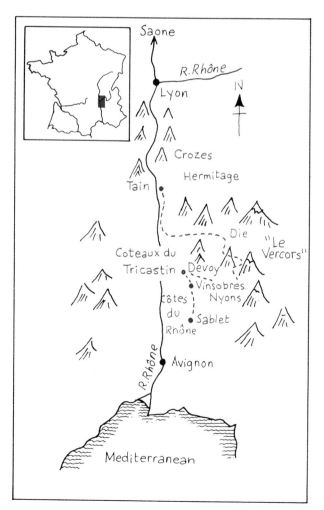

I left the warmth of Sablet (near Orange in the southern Rhône valley) early and by midday was up in the snows of Alpine foothills. My plan was to take in the east bank of the top half of the Rhône valley, what the French call the *Septentrional* as opposed to the *Méridional* part. I wanted to include at least one further Côtes du Rhône Village—there are 14 or so on the east bank and all different … but not that different. So, having done Sablet, Rasteau and Cairanne I decided to go one step north and look at Vinsobres. Jean Ezingeard was a small, square man who had only recently left the local cooperative with his partner/neighbour Jean Benoit, to bottle his own. The results were superb; possibly because of the vineyard's location in a climatically favoured little side valley. Vinsobres is generally held to share the characteristics of Southern Rhône (fruity Grenache) and Northern Rhône (Syrah—dark and perfumy). Aussellons was also well worth finding.

Monsieur Ezingeard
Domaine des Aussellons
Villedieu, 84110 Vaison la Romaine
(Vaucluse)

Then farewell Côtes du Rhône, hello Coteaux du Tricastin. Tricastin is a new appellation, an area of much less intensive but not negligible wine growing lying to the north of the Côtes du Rhône.

It only came into official being in 1970 as a VDQS but was rapidly promoted to AOC status.

Imagine you are Pierre Bouat-Labeye, a farmer of sugarbeet in the Pas de Calais (the flat, dull bit just after the ferry). You chuck it all in, go south and persuade the Hunting Club of Donzère to sell you a hundred acres of worthless scrub woodland alongside the A6 motorway south of Montélimar. You bulldoze down all the trees, push the odd annoying little hillock into the odd awkward little ravine and get … a vast acreage of

prime cobblestones! Your friends from Calais come to see you and end up backing away, speaking soothingly before phoning the hospital. You have created a sort of Brighton beach, only bigger and … (here is the clue) apparently identical to the soil of a certain wine area called Châteauneuf-du-Pape. You invest a fortune in vineyards, sow rows a mile long and buy big machines to turn over your cobblestones every so often. Then, your eccentricity still not satisfied, you build yourself a space-age tower in which to make your wine. Far from being a cosy, folksy cellar, with cobwebs and old casks this is something more Cape Canaveral. Imported from

California, the idea is realized in a set of pivoting steel vats exposed to the elements for coolness, through which the fermenting wine passes by gravity alone from top to bottom, controlled by just one man. With his vast, flat vineyard and his tower, Pierre can achieve the work of twenty men with just three. It is a touch soul-less, but very clever and economic. The vine varieties are Grenache and Syrah with which he makes blends using more or less of either. The pure young Syrah wine is black, very concentrated and tannic; the Grenache is light in colour and body, but lovely and fruity. We liked the blend of 60 per cent Syrah with 40 per cent Grenache; whilst expensive because Syrah is dear, it was nevertheless undoubtedly his best balanced blend.

Pierre Bovat-Labeye
Domaine de la Tour d'Elyssas
26290 Donzère

Then I headed for the hills up the River Eygues, passing through Nyon, a nice sheltered corner where olive trees have survived the 1956 frost that killed most of those found throughout the Rhône. Moving into the Baronnies on the minor D61 road I encountered high country and poor land. My intention was to get over into the Drôme valley and the isolated little Shangri-la of the Diois. Here snow capped mountains, pinewoods and wild, wild country characterized the scene. The Vercors—heartland of the French Resistance throughout the Occupation—was now filled just with shepherds and their mixed herds of sheep and goats. I travelled on to Die—snug in its little valley beneath its very own mountain—and the impressive story of the Clairette.

After the war there was a little bit of wine grown here and there, mostly white, cheap and often acidic. It is often the case that where you get cheap, acid wine people fizz it up to make it taste better. They may not quite phrase it that way in their publicity brochures, but in a nutshell that is exactly what happened in Champagne, Saumur, Limoux and all the rest—happily. In Die a few friends decided to pool resources and cooperate: making fizzy wine is a very expensive process, and all that liquid investment going 'bubble, bubble' costs. They also decided to promote the little known Muscat grape which was a huge success. Now Clairette de Die (made not from Clairette at all, but Muscat) is their most popular wine. I

Jean-Claude... or his twin brother!

suppose it is related to the Muscats of Asti but it seems much classier somehow.

Now, I started out with the serious intention of telling you all about the magnificent enterprise that has grown out of those early beginnings: the acres of bottles, private railway track, the clever machines, the hospitable tasting room built like a church. But ... this wine is just not so *sérieux*. Just drink it one warm summer's afternoon with a close friend. You'll see. I also recommend a bottle of true, dry, Clairette for aperitif-going-on-to-the-meal sort of use: Cuvée des Voconces is one of my favourites.

Châtillon-en-Diois
Cave Coopérative de Die
Avenue de la Clairette, 25160 Die

Just a bit up the valley, part of the same region really but clinging stubbornly to its independence, is the little wine area of Châtillon-en-Diois. They grow tiny amounts of still red wine in a patch of vineyards no bigger than a dozen football pitches, clustered at the foot of a vast rock wall that towers to the skies. The neat vineyards, like allotments, each have a similarly neat little stone hut for the tools, the siesta and who-knows-what. The Châtillonais are mountain people: energetic, very tough and hardworking. The town of Châtillon is very huddled with only two streets and lots of dark alleyways. I ate at the Hôtel de France which turned out to be my favourite sort of French restaurant with its pervading 20's atmosphere. The town banker, doctor, teacher and mechanic were all eating as they had done every day of their lives; blue overalls and dark suits mixed together and they ate at prices that defy the laws of economics. A large hyper-motherly *Madame* pounces on small Number Two son and carts him off for compulsory admiration by the *clientèle* and kitchen staff. He returns, shaken and is quiet for the rest of the day. When you are ten months old I suppose a bosom that ample must be as threatening as an approaching avalanche.

Despite it being mid-January the snow held off, and driving was easy, back down into the warmth of the Rhône valley at Loriol. There are virtually no vines along this bit, so I drove north about a half hour until the unmistakable hill of Hermitage hoved into view. At the bottom of the slope, one allotment-size patch (not that you usually get allotments on a one-in-one slope) belongs to my man Fayolle. It used to be 'my man', now it's 'my men' Fayolle, the Père Jules having retired and handed over to *Les fils*— identical twins Jean-Claude and Jean-Paul.

Between you and me, I am much relieved as Jules was a bit of an old beggar to deal with. A peasant of the old school was Jules. Earthy. Likewise his cellar and his wines. His sons still make 'wines made the old way', but without quite the extremes that Jules favoured. But he was always honest and made concentrated wines with lots of grapes per bottle. And he was always meticulous in his cellar, even if it was the oddest collection of old barrels you ever saw. Bottlings, however, were sometimes left a bit too much to nature, and nature unfortunately sometimes took a wrong course. This just goes to prove that technology does not go amiss in the finishing of a wine.

Jules Fayolle et ses Fils
Gervans (Drôme)
26600 Tain l'Hermitage

The twins have been to agricultural college, though I still expect to see them up to their waists in the old wood fermenters treading the floating mat of grapeskins. But I know they exercise their heads also, and we already see brighter wine in the bottles. The sons each owned a house in the village, one at the bottom, and one at the top amongst the vines. But their father hung on to the family home above the cellars. This proved inconvenient and in the Autumn of 1983 came 'Le Grand Evénement'. At 2am on November 20th Père Fayolle rose from his bed and, with the habit of a lifetime, descended to a very small room by the back-door. As the door banged shut, there came a rumbling, a shaking and shuddering, and by the light of the full moon Jules, aghast, in beret and pyjamas watched half of his house (the old part, non-inhabited) slide gracefully down into the cellars below. He dropped what he was doing but it was far too late. Half the barrels in his cellar were gone and a stream of red ran down the road toward the village. Four days later Jules and Yvette left their old home. Jean-Paul and his family moved in. A new era. The cellar is rebuilt already but concrete is not quite the same as those blackened old stones. However, now at least there is room on top for new farm buildings.

The Fayolle cellar is at Gervans, a couple of miles north of Tain in the region of Crozes Hermitage. Their little one hectare plot of Hermitage Les Dioinnières is an ambition I suspect Jules cherished all his arduous life as he tended those terrible steep slopes of his. He acquired his Hermitage just before he retired. The Hermitage wine costs twice as much as is usual for Crozes and it is not twice the wine. But after tasting the different *climats* of Crozes—the Pontaix, the Voussères and so on you are certainly aware that you have gone up a league when you try the one vat of Hermitage that sits apart. Red Crozes and red Hermitage are planted solely with the Syrah, a popular grape, planted elsewhere these days from Adelaide to Napa. The white wines are made with Marsanne, which so far has not progressed beyond Rhône. It is an odd wine in

that it is a white with so many of the characteristics of a red that you must be careful not to serve it in a dark dining room!

All three of these wines from Fayolle should ideally be kept a good few years—they are virtually indestructible.

I must also tell you about a nice white Hermitage which I acquired from a friend of a friend. Jean-Louis Chave is one of a tiny select group of progressive Rhône valley wine-makers who meet and share out their knowledge. André Roux, another member, told me about Jean-Louis and served me his white Hermitage at dinner. It is a revelation, similar to the Crozes white but altogether finer.

Domaine Chave
Mauves, 07300 Tournon-sur-Rhône

—STAGE 6—
Beaujolais

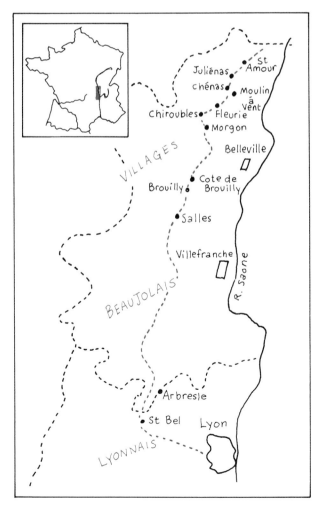

I was motoring up the Rhône valley looking over at the remainder of the Rhône vineyards on the west bank which I have not yet visited. Between them and my next port of call, Beaujolais, lies Lyon. I read somewhere that Lyon used to have considerable vineyards right in the centre of town, and there is still supposed to be a Vin du Lyonnais. I checked out the reference books and discovered a cooperative wine cellar just in the outer suburbs at a place called Saint Bel. I poled up there to find a wine cooperative much like any other in France. It had a nice little shop, teeming with people out from Lyon filling car boots with bottles and refilled Bag-in-Boxes. The friendly 'directeur' greeted us, somewhat puzzled to meet a would-be foreign buyer. As far as he knew they had never exported.

Cave Coopérative des Coteaux du Lyonnais
Saint Bel, 69210 L'Arbresle

I tried the wine they were offering all passers-by which was their red Coteaux du Lyonnais. It was made — surprise, surprise — with the Gamay grape of Beaujolais fame. One sip and I felt I could fling my cap in the air and cry 'whoopee'. My optimistic mind told me that it was another Bergerac. Bergerac is to Bordeaux, as Lyonnais is to Beaujolais — very similar, but cheaper. But I remained hard-faced, I mean I was supposed to be a business man. If I had cried

'whoopee' it would have been a franc more. The price was good, two thirds that of the Beaujolais from the next-commune-but-one to the north. I would defy anyone to tell the difference.

As I drove on north, I scarcely saw any vines. It was pasture mostly with some corn until just past L'Arbresle. There, all of a sudden ... vines everywhere — Beaujolais. This must surely be the happiest of wines and the jolliest of regions with its big, rolling hills, vines, woods and houses. We went on north to Pont des Samsons and encountered some 21st century wine making. The Beaujolais Producteurs used to be a funny little outfit operating in what I took to be a converted garage. Now they have a vast building with more stainless steel than Cape Canaveral. As the central bottling plant for most of the big cooperative cellars of Beaujolais, they have a lot to bottle.

Sica Beaujolais Producteurs
Départementale 37 'Le Pont des Samsons'
Quincié en Beaujolais
69430 Beaujeu

Roland Micouin, the resident oenologist, bright, young, bearded and agile, showed me round, leaping from vat to vat with little whoops of enthusiasm for all the lovely 1982's, especially for the better wines, for the bigger tougher wines which needed more time to mature and were not sold as *nouveau*. After a mammoth tasting I chose a few vats of Cru Villages wine from those villages where this organization has a cellar. There were some lovely wines but we will come to those later. The main reason I came here was because these are the obvious people to go to for an outstanding basic Beaujolais. They have the size, resources and economies of scale. I rarely buy basic Beaujolais, preferring Villages which are always much bigger wines and not that much dearer. But I picked a pear-droppy purple number which I considered a perfect example for illustrating just what fun this stuff should be.

Charentay was the next stop, where I saw André Jaffre who makes a magnificent Beaujolais Villages and Primeur (he pronounces it 'Primor'). André is a great friend and introduced me to many of the other Beaujolais people mentioned later.

André Jaffre
Domaine du Chêne
Charentay

It was now time to prepare for one of the most delightful wine journeys in the world, the 'Route du Beaujolais' as it winds its way through all nine Cru Village appellations. By Odenas I was already in the southernmost: Brouilly. Six communes make up Brouilly, a doughnut shaped area around the base of Mont Brouilly. Those vineyards on the Mont itself, the Côte de Brouilly, are blessed with volcanic, granite-based soils and consider themselves very much above those lower down with their clay/limestone rubbish! Côtes de Brouillys are considered the 'gold top' versions of Brouilly which is characterized by a special, light grapiness. I find a pepperiness too. Lucien Verger was pruning vines by the roadside, wasting no time as he waited for my arrival. A big, dark, powerful man who looks frightening when cross (and I once made him cross). He is a *métayer* or a share cropper — not unusual in Beaujolais. The land is not his but he farms it in return for half the crop going to the landlord.

Lucien Verger
c/o Un Eventail de Vignerons Producteurs
Corcelles-en-Beaujolais
69220 Belleville

Lucien has eight hectares of vines in a prime spot halfway up Mont Brouilly with a marvellous view facing full south. Some of his wine is Côte de Brouilly, some Brouilly, but as I tasted freezing-cold young examples from the vats I must confess to having been unable to differentiate. With his cellars being nearly 1,000 feet up, he has problems cold-starting his fermentations. So before proper harvesting, he has to get a little tub of grapejuice fermenting away in the warmth of his kitchen; when that is bubbling merrily it is tipped into the first vat as a 'starter' and known as a *pied de cuve*. Each new vat is then 'started' by a bucketful of the one that went before. Like most of the Beaujolais the grapes drop into the vats from the top, uncrushed — they are semi-macerated. Lucien's cellar is on a slope with two levels of access to facilitate this.

At Morgon I met Louis Genillon. Morgon is the easy one to remember. It is the tough

Beaujolais. That night as I sampled from Louis's 100-year-old silver tastevin, it seemed more Pinot Noir than Gamay, and more like a young Burgundy from the Côte d'Or than a flippantly fruity Beaujolais. Morgon along with other Villages wines thought to be similar are said to

Lucien Verger - Brouilly.

'morgonne'. Only the locals know precisely what that means but it is something to do with being firmer, less showy when young and needing more time to ripen. You certainly do not drink 'Morgon Nouveau'.

Louis Genillon
c/o Un Eventail de Vignerons Producteurs
Corcelles-en-Beaujolais
69220 Belleville

I stayed the night in Salles, at a crazy, rambling guest house, run by two ladies, one of whom I believe is boss and the other servant. Or they could be sisters. Then I proceeded to Mademoiselle Chabert. Do you remember Mademoiselle from Fleurie? On BBC 1's 'Year of the French'? 'Queen of the Beaujolais'? I went to see Marguerite in her little front parlour on the High Street in Fleurie, next to the family charcuterie where I dutifully bought *Andouillettes de Fleurie*. She lives alone in her little house and has presided over the cooperative down the road for over thirty years since her father fell ill.

Running a French cooperative must be one of the toughest jobs on earth; Frenchmen do not naturally cooperate, so she really is some Queen. She was up in arms at having to send half the beautiful, but over-bountiful 1982 crop to the distillery. Some people, you see, produced a

phenomenal 100 hectolitres a hectare. Mind you I expect there will be the usual rapid 'evaporation' before the inspectors come to get it. She offered me 1979 and 1973 to show how well a light Beaujolais like Fleurie does age. She has many good bottles from the 1920's and 30's. So it is clear that you need not rush this wine even though its light clay soils make it the lightest of the Crus. I left her in her parlour, making off with not only a lovely Fleurie 1982, but also the best Chiroubles I found during my stay. Chiroubles is a small village squeezed between Morgon, Fleurie and the high mountains. The wine is very similar to Fleurie in style; 'light and luscious'.

Cave de Fleurie
69820 Fleurie

The next place is Moulin-à-Vent, 'King of the Crus' with its manganese-rich volcanic soil which is said to make the darkest, strongest, biggest, toughest and most *sérieux* of Beaujolais. But in fact it is not really Beaujolais at all, rather a red Burgundy in need of a few years keeping. Chénas the next Cru along makes very similar wines, which are just a touch less weighty. I got both Moulin-à-Vent and Chénas from the cooperative at Chénas who now own the Château de Chénas.

Château de Chénas
Chénas
69840 Juliénas

There were just two Crus to go and these were my favourites: Juliénas and right in the north, the romantic sounding Saint Amour! Juliénas is the wine they say 'you either like or you don't like'. It is uncompromising, strong, sinewy stuff (not fat and fruity) and is supposed to be easy to pick out at tastings, but not by me. André Pelletier is the comedian who makes the one I tasted. He is a lovely man who loves life; he used to be a *métayer* but now has his own steep little four and a half hectare plot. I like a man who will retain the old manual wine presses because he would rather have all the riotousness and gaiety of his student harvesters than cold hydraulic efficiency. I like, too, the way his father at 84 is still sent out pruning; you have to get a return on your OAPs these days!

André Pelletier
Les Foullouses
69840 Juliénas

And lastly in Saint Amour, I settled down to Jean Pâtissier's wine that I have loved for years. Most 'Primeurish' of the Crus, it has a crocus-like ability always to be the first to flower. I marvelled that it was so rounded, so seductively fruity. Old Jean has split up his vines (he is *métayer* on 10 hectares belonging to a Madame Ladville) with two of his sons. Although the *mauvaises langues* told me, 'the old sod won't risk being outshone so he gave his sons the worst vines!' I could taste very little difference between the casks marked 'Jean', 'Jean Bernard', 'Guy' or 'Ladville' in their cellar. My notes read: 'all lovely mouth explosion; still a few bubbles, touch of green' and '*corsé* but overwhelmingly lovely.' It was a high note on which to end an exhaustive and exhausting *étape*.

André Pelletier syphoning from a barrel.

The Mâconnais and Chalonnais

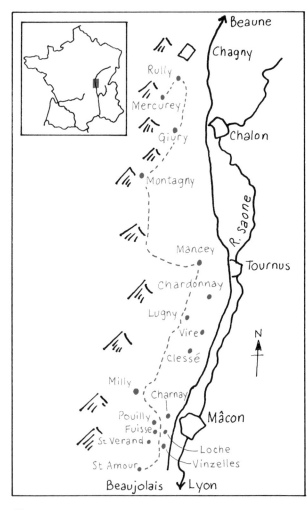

THE wine areas around Mâcon and Chalon — the Mâconnais and Chalonnais — will not appreciate being lumped together. (Fierce Burgundian pride!) However, I must be practical and — I might as well come clean about this — I have not found the time even on this trek to linger long in this area. Until now in Mâcon I have really only ever needed one address, that of Bernard Meunier. Sadly, however, he died in the summer of 1982 and I lost the man who taught me all about southern Burgundy.

Bernard ran the cooperative group now called 'Bourgignons Producteurs' which comprises virtually all the cooperatives in this lower-middle part of Burgundy. Thus he was able — and indeed the group still is — to offer the full range from Pouilly Fuissé down to basic Mâcon Blanc — all of it very good. And I do not say that lightly. It is, I think, a verifiable fact that an almost unique particularity of the Mâconnais is the way the cooperatives totally dominate the region. They are not only large and numerous but also, according to the results of the *concours* (and Mâcon itself hosts the top *Concours de Vins* of France) they make the best wines. The *caves* of Prissé, Lugny, and Sologny, etc, always run off with the medals. So ... my account of the trek to the Mâconnais is simple; turn left at the top end of Beaujolais where St-Amour's red Beaujolais is

The Mâconnais in winter.

A view of the Chalonnais.

actually intertwined with St-Veran's white Burgundy, and visit the cooperative at Charnay-lès-Mâcon. Here I found the central cooperative of the group and a mammoth tasting of all the 1982 wines as well as what was left of the superb 1981s. I finally settled on five wines.

UCVB (Union des Coopératives Vinicoles de Bourgogne)
Charnay-lès-Mâcon
71008 Mâcon Cedex

Aligoté is usually so acid that it hurts your teeth but this sunny 1982 vintage was round, soft and lovely. The Mâcon Village whites were fine and very full in 1982 but were better by autumn. I grabbed, meanwhile, all they had left of their superb 1981. The St-Véran I tasted should be considered like gold top Mâcon Villages. It is a relatively recent AOC designed to give a real name to the excellent white wines made in northern Beaujolais. There is no actual place called St-Véran. Then further up the scale came a huge great Pouilly Vinzelles and an even more massive Pouilly Fuissé. These wines were so dense they were hard to swirl. I do exaggerate, of course, but just wish to convey that it is their concentration that makes the wines great — and expensive. 1982 was really a keeping vintage, (not enough acidity) but these two needed a year or two at least.

As for reds, I have always found the Mâcon product, be it Gamay or Pinot too 'hard' most years. 1982 was of course, an exception. With all that sun the Gamay grape (Mâcon), the Pinot grape (Bourgogne) and the 'mixed' Passe toutgrains all became exceptionally good.

That is it really, though I also went to visit Lamartine's house in Milly. I could not actually get inside but was consoled by a super meal in the café across the road. It was run by a nice, keen, young couple who were very idealistic about traditional, local food. They served it cheaply in an authentic (scruffy) bar setting. They also coped amazingly with the four infants I seemed to have acquired; plate after plate of *frites* on the side is worth three stars to me! I promised I would tell everyone to go and eat there, so scrub round a Michelin-starred blowout — such youthful ideals must be supported — and try 'Chez Jack' at Milly-Lamartine.

The northern Mâconnais blends imperceptibly into the Chalonnais. Green rolling fields lie dotted with vast Burgundian farmhouses. In fact it is quite difficult to decide when a farm is not a farm but a manor or a château. They are all rather grand and imposing with the characteristic large verandahs on the first floor. Every now and then a particularly felicitous site sports a vineyard or two, usually a sheltered slope, or a *cuvette*. But it is very unlike Beaujolais with its all-over vines; there are definitely more cows than vines here. Chardonnay, presumably the village that gave its name to the world famous grape, is an attractive place as are Lugny and Viré. Mancey, however, the northern-most Mâcon village, is less pretty but boasts a small cooperative cellar with a chaotic and overwhelmingly enthusiastic director — Bernard Derain. I preferred his basic Mâcon red to the others I tried. The method used is partially *macération carbonique* and therefore the wine was bigger and softer than most.

Cave de Vignerons de Mancey
71240 Sennecey-Le-Grand

As I seem to have said I noticed no perceptible change moving into the Chalonnais. I travelled on past lovely châteaux like Sercey and Saule to Montagny, which straggles prettily around the rim of its small bowl of vineyards comprising only about 120 hectares. There I met young Alain Le Roy, a highly-qualified, young, keen wine-maker who had just taken over his parents' eight hectares. I tried several vats, and liked the 1981 in vat 12 that had a perfect balance between green acid and full fatness producing a wine which is both refreshing and substantial. It had a hint of hazelnut and, as Alain said, of flint. He says his wines have more flavour than most because he keeps them *sur lie* (on the sediment) as they do in Muscadet.

The cellars of the cooperative at Lugny.

château de la Saule
Montagny

Domaine Roy
Château de la Saule, Montagny-les-Buxy
71390 Buxy

I continued on my way to a friend of Le Roy's at Givry. Maurice Derain at Moroges is a third generation, very typical Burgundian grower with five hectares on the best *coteau* up at Russilly. Givry's are the toughest of Chalonnais reds; thick soils make hard wines and Givry is dense clay.

Chez De Launay
Mercurey.

They all seem keen to tell you that their wine was the one preferred by Henri IV (their Henry IV, not ours). But then they say the same thing from Jurançon to Puisseguin — he must have been some drinker!

Maurice Derain
71390 Buxy

Monsieur de Launay's place at Mercurey was the next port of call. I say 'Monsieur' because I have not plucked up the courage to use his christian name yet. This very tall, angular aristocratic man sports a Lincoln beard and owns fierce gun dogs. His two-year-old and mine hit it off well though (with the emphasis on the 'hit') so I have hopes of long-term links with the de Launays. He was out pruning in a bitter east wind when we arrived, but we adjourned inside round a huge log fire for a memorable tasting. The white 1982s had still not finished doing their thing in the barrels below so we stuck to a 1981. It was not cheap thanks to a lot of hail damage in 1981, and only 7% of Mercurey vines (usually the higher ones) are white anyway — Chardonnay of course. The wine is similar to a Rully white (see below) but more *trappu* (as they say) which I think means more solid. It takes its time to 'open'. The red 1980s were almost ready-to-drink and I fell for the expensive one (alas) grown within the walled Clos du Château de Montaigu, right next to the house. It is amazing what an eight foot surrounding wall does to a vineyard's micro-climate; in this case it makes a much more substantial wine which is dark, solid and fine.

Paul and Yves de Launay
Domaine de Launay
Clos du Château de Montaigu
Mercurey
71640 Givry

I have been visiting one particular *cave* in Rully for ages. Jean-François Delorme, probably one of the nicest men in the game, runs his family's large sparkling Burgundy business and their Chalonnais vineyards. He makes the best-known of Rullys. The red is always a lightweight alongside its Côte d'Or brothers, but most years come packed with a fine Pinot Noir flavour. I enjoyed a comprehensive tasting of all the Chalonnais wines over several vintages. I decided his red 1981s were too hard and too expensive; the red 1980s and 1982s were much friendlier wines and were round and ready to drink now. I plumped finally for the Domaine de la Renarde 1980 Rully. (I noted down that it made me think of a little old lady — lavender, violets, velvet and lace.) A mouth filling, full, white Rully Varot also caught my nose. It was very pungent and very fine.

Jean-François Delorme
Domaine de la Renarde
Caves Delorme-Meulieu
Rully 71150 Chagny

—STAGE 8—
Top of the Loire

HAVING 'done' the vineyards around Chalon I headed west over the hills of Morvan to the Loire. A journey from one warm, wealthy, fertile valley, via cool, poor, forested uplands to another warm, wealthy, fertile valley. The upland break is good for you, like skipping a meal when travelling in France. I found cool green forests and pasture with sheep, no vines and nothing lush.

Château Chinon is François Mitterand's constituency. The town fountain does not work! There are lots of potteries along the way belonging to real old-fashioned producers of *grés* (rough brown-glazed ware). They make those huge pots used for *confit* (preserving goosemeat in goose fat); I always make a habit of loading up with rejects at amazing prices. My other habit when driving across France and not too *pressé* is to draw a straight line between departure and destination and try to stay on it. French secondary roads are so good and straight compared to our own; there is much less traffic, especially lorries; and the countryside seems fresher somehow. This way you also feel you are discovering views no Briton can have seen before.

The only problem is the lethal *priorité à droite* that allows any hick farmhand on a tractor to charge out from concealed entrances. If you hit him it is your fault ... provided he came in from the right. I find this a difficult system to get used to. I have a clear memory of passing through what is really the last village of this trek just before getting to the Loire ... maybe seven years ago? Luckily I was being cautious as I cruised gently down the street watching my *droite*. Suddenly 'SHRIEK!' a white torpedo about eighteen feet long shot across my bows with only inches to spare. It was one of those new-fangled pigs (the

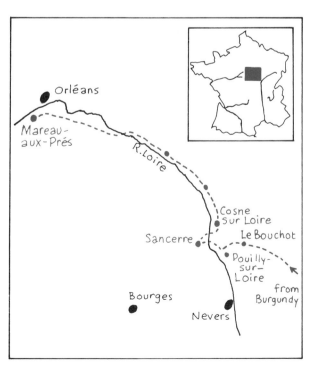

The village of Chavignol near Sancerre.

stretched version with a hundred teats and highly efficient). Now highly cross, she raced ahead of me and vanished, as I nosed painfully into my windscreen. Not a soul was around but had I hit the old sow they would have been swarming. After all she came from the right! French logic.

I arrived at Pouilly-sur-Loire home of the celebrated Pouilly Fumé. The unwary often mix it up with Pouilly Fuissé, which is a white Burgundy-Chardonnay grape grown near Mâcon; this on the other hand is 'Smoked Pouilly' and it is made from Sauvignon Blanc grapes on the banks of the Loire, just downstream from Nevers. Call it Pouilly Blanc Fumé if you wish, you will impress your friends no end and possibly avoid future confusions.

This smoked business is a taste in the wine said to derive from the local soil. There is another British wine merchant who goes on a fair bit about the clays and all that, so I will leave well alone; Mr Yapp has cornered the Kimmeridge business. Suffice to say that this smoky aroma is one that I, personally, find extremely hard to distinguish.

My suppliers in Pouilly, or rather in the

Always tasting, always testing.

hamlet of Le Bouchot on the ridge above it, are the Séguin family — mother, father Raymond, son, and daughter-in-law. When I first found them the son was still at college, and they just had a tiny house with a tiny old cellar underneath. Last time I visited, son Hervé had built his new bungalow on top of a vast new concrete cellar, and they are geared up to a substantial production in bottle. The feel is still quite *artisanale* though. The cellar floor always seems covered with hundreds of bottles resulting from lengthy evenings of hand bottling, labelling, capsuling and boxing. I confess to feeling conceited pride on going down into some little cellar like this, lost in France, to see pallets of cartons all neatly labelled 'Bordeaux Direct, Reading, Angleterre'. Even if, like this house, I get my ear bent with: 'when are your xxxxxxx *transporteurs* finally coming to collect, we can't move with this lot in the hallway?'

Raymond, Hervé e a few bottles 'chez Séguin'

Séguin Père et Fils
Le Bouchot
58150 Pouilly-sur-Loire, Nièvre

The year that I visited, almost for the first time, the bumper harvest had given the Séguins enough produce to sell me some of the region's second wine, Pouilly-sur-Loire. Locally, this is considered a less sérieux drink, but one that anywhere else would be lauded to the skies. Made from Chasselas grapes (which are also table grapes) it does need a good hot year to be truly nice, and this particular year it was hot enough. At the bottom of the hill, in Pouilly itself is the Cave Coopérative. Opposite is the Coq Hardi restaurant of the Relais Fleurie. A difficult choice but the Relais won. I had a lovely lunch in the

Machines cannot replace the care
and attention these vines receive.

wintry sunshine; outside, gardeners were pruning the *fleurie* bit (a rose-encrusted pergola) that must be nice for those who do not have to do their French travelling in the winter.

Beyond the meadow a very swollen Loire flowed fast by. Cows chewed; willows showed first green; cowslips popped up and I ate fresh trout, thinking — this is the life! After lunch the cooperative seemed worth a visit. I was flattered to be remembered by Bernard Bouchier the *directeur* because I have not bought here for ten years. It just so happened that he had a little lot of 100 cases of the local red wine Coteaux du Giennois: Domaine du Château de Saint Péré. I saw the boxes sitting a bit forlorn in the middle of the cellar. A Paris merchant had let him down. This was clearly a chance for a haggle. He obviously wanted them out of the way and their bottle-age — look at the dust! — appealed to me. I tried not to show it and tasted a bottle. It reminded me uncannily of strawberry — actually de-frosted strawberry — not acid-fresh but a bit mushy.

Domaine du Château de Saint Péré
Cave Coopérative Pouilly-sur-Loire
58150 Pouilly-sur-Loire

I drove north up the N7 toward Cosne-sur-Loire where the Giennois red is grown. Then I veered off left and went over the river to Sancerre, Pouilly's twin sister. My friend Pierre Riffault lives at Les Egrots, a tiny hamlet near Sury-en-Vaux. Pierre is another one with a new cellar; he also has a lovely wine again, though the vats vary. I dared to disagree which was best, but then I have known Pierre many years. He comes to the UK a fair bit ... dancing ... with a local folk dance group 'La Sabotée Sancerroise' which means 'The Cloggies of Sancerre' ... no kidding! From his goat-herding granny he gets Crottins de Chavignol, the other local appellation — for cheese! About the size of a small scone, it has a mouldy blue outside, a crumbly white inside and is often served warm, or even better toasted. It is particularly delicious with cold, fresh-grassy Sancerre ... heaven. At the end of his row of spotless vats Pierre has a few spotless old barrels for the rosé made from his Pinot Noir. Some Sancerre growers make their Pinot more as a red, but it is never a real red compared to Burgundy. I prefer to call a spade a spade ... and therefore say

Chez Riffault.

it is a rosé. Normally I would not buy any, though I love drinking it. The social stigma of rosé is such a problem in Britain where they call it the 'cop-out' wine. But on my trek I am doing every wine region, *thoroughly* — and this is a 1982 yet again (l'année merveille) that I could not and did not resist. Serve Pierre's dark rosé cellar-cold as a delicious summer lunch wine and savour the unmistakable wicked Pinot aroma.

Pierre Riffault
Les Egrots
Sury-en-Vaux
18300 Sancerre

Orléans (Joan-of-Arc's place) has always puzzled me; like Lyon, it is a large and illogical gap in the viticultural map. Excellent wines are grown along the Loire either side of Orléans, so why not just there? I had heard mention of 'Vin d'Orléans', but what colour was it and where could one find it? It turns out there are three cooperative wineries, one in such desperate straits it is about to close, and four independent growers. I ended up at Mareau-aux-Prés a 140-member cooperative which farm 190 hectares (quite sizable). One problem seems to be the encroachment of the city suburbs on the vineyards. Vines like a nice south-facing slope looking over the river. So too, it seems, do

The canal at Sancerre.

accountants, insurance salesmen, bank managers and assorted merchants. And unfortunately bungalows earn more than vines. The other problem is the dear growers themselves. I was royally received by the president and vice president (I was only the second foreign merchant ever seen here) but alas my enthusiasm must have shown; for when I came to order a month later, a staggering, previously unmentioned 20% price increase had happened and, no matter how much I yelled, stuck.

What had attracted my interest was their white; their red Gamay was far too green. And though their Pinot Meunier 'grey' wine is well worth trying (locally they treat it as a red), I really fell for that dry white! It says on the label that it is made from a grape called Blanc Auvergnat. Some weird plant from the Massif Central, I thought. 'Oh,' said those two cunning peasants, all innocent-like and fooling me completely, 'that vine does have another name; around here they sometimes call it er … Chardonnay!' As I choked in my cup at the thought of an undiscovered source of cheap Chardonnay, the world's most popular grape (you can get pounds a bottle from Americans for Chardonnay), that was when the cunning, conning peasants mentally put their price up.

Cave Coopérative de Mareau-aux-Prés
45370 Cléry Saint André.

Sancerre.

—STAGE 9—
Touraine

AT last after four months I have come to a reasonably priced wine region. All that Burgundy and Upper Loire stuff is all very well 'mais alors, on est vite bankrupt.' Although Touraine *per se,* is pretty well known these days for its cheap Gamays and Sauvignons, a lot of its odd corners remain hidden, and on the basis of my little journey's results, that is a shame. The wines on this track are, I am sure, eventually destined to become regular favourites, on *my* wine list at least.

I was in Orléans, you might recall. I descended from there down the river to Blois. Blois has a famous château and in a dungeon of this landmark I once participated in a strange ritual. Every year, around Easter time, the wine growers of the Chéverny VDQS district assemble to taste and vote upon each other's wine for purposes of awarding *Les Labels.* These are the little numbered stamps you see reproduced on all VDQS labels. They denote that the stuff is authentic and that it has been tasted by this assembly and found (a) drinkable (b) typical. Every VDQS area does this, AOC areas do not.

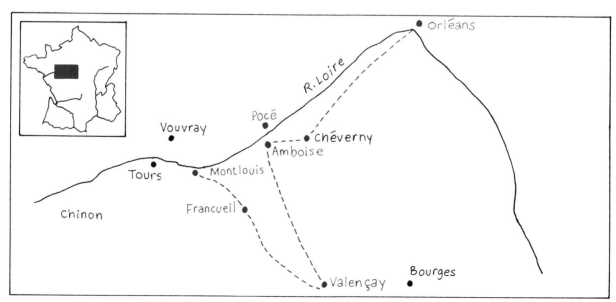

Appellation d'Origine Contrôlée is presumably thought to be so irreproachably good that it does not need checking every year. (What a mistake!) By the way, there is an interesting new ruse come into being lately: VDQS growers desirous of improving their image now put on their labels one line that says *Appellation d'Origine,* then a second saying *Vin Délimité de Qualité Supérieur.* So what is it — AOC or VDQS? It is the latter; without the 'Controlled' bit, the name of origin means nothing.

Anyway, there was a gathering of about fifty farmers; good, ruddy-faced, be-bereted *paysans* grasping in their dinner-plate hands wee little tumblers of the fresh white Chéverny … *de l'Année.* It was none of your frightfully hushed, frightfully pinstripe, frightfully *sérieux* London wine trade tastings. Nor was it your sip-gargle-spit-write-short-essay-using-same-six-adjectives. No, this was obviously 'A Big Day in Chéverny'. And not a lot happens in Chéverny I would say, since Robespierre shut down the big house. They were here today for a party. The noise level was dangerous after five minutes and punctuated by great hoots of laughter and jibes. 'Errgh … this must be Jacko's wine … EH JACKO cat got in the cellar again?' It must be admitted that Chéverny can be a tart wine. The Romorantin grape from which the wine is made is a little-known local varietal that needs a good deal of sun, otherwise … ouch! Like Gros Plant it is said to be sponsored by the French Dental Association.

The tasting got rowdier while I got more confused. The sample bottles were identified solely by number, so it was a blindfold do. But as the bottles were passed around everywhere, less and less attention seemed to be paid to the numbers. Nobody wrote much, I doubt if some could write. I was only there as a casual observer with a friend, Pierre Chainier, and so left early, but I still have this strong mental image. There in the middle of this rustic throng was a painted lady complete with scarlet lips, rouge, black dress, Bloomsbury group big black hat and feather boa. Who on earth? 'She used to play piano for Josephine Baker!' After a lifetime of touring the US jazz clubs, she had come back here to retire and grow wine! I felt sure that after we left, Mademoiselle Baker's friend would be dragged to a piano and the *Comité de Dégustation* would jolly on all night. Everything would be drunk; nothing would be noted down; and everyone would get their *Labels.* But that is only my fanciful theory. I am sure the reality is far more *sérieux* … and boring.

My guide then was Pierre Chainier, a young successful wine merchant based in Amboise who has now, amongst other things, organized a group of growers in different districts of Touraine to form an association for the purpose of bottling their own wine with his new mobile bottling plant. I like this plan. The grower watches over his own wine until it is safely bottled, can use very sophisticated sterile bottling equipment that fragile white wines in particular badly need, yet

Amboise

he does not have the impossible expense of actually having to buy the machinery for his little smallholding. Touraine is not a region of big estates. The Chéverny member of Pierre's group makes a crisp, leafy, vegetal, dry white that is terrific value as an all-purpose fish accompaniment. Another participant in the *groupement* is Yves Seneau. His Domaine du Grand Moulin made the loveliest Sauvignon Blanc I saw that year … and because I placed importance on having a good Sauvignon Blanc I visited no less than ten other cellars before picking this one. The 1982 'miracle vintage' appears to have been at its least miraculous for Sauvignons because the intense heat boiled away their flavour. But Châteauvieux is as good as any you will have tried … of *any* vintage.

Monsieur Bernard Cazin
Domaine Le Petit Chambord,
Chéverny, 41700 Contres

Domaine du Grand Moulin
Châteauvieux
Loir-et-Cher

Pierre Chainier has also managed to acquire his own vineyard as a result of his success. It is called Château de Pocé; it lies on the north bank of the Loire, and it used to be an orphanage! The rambling old château must have been a bit draughty and ominous for the poor inmates, but now they are re-lodged in beautiful new family houses in woods about the estate. The vineyard which is the largest in the district is planted with Gamay — the Beaujolais grape. It is made in caverns cut in the rock directly below the vines and turned out to be a very agreeable, juicy gulping red when I tried it.

Château de Pocé
Pocé-sur-Cisse

Valençay is in Berry rather than Touraine and you have to drive through a lot of old hunting forest to get there. Just down the road from the great château, the local cooperative makes wine from all the typical varieties: Gamay, Sauvignon, etc. I liked their Cabernet best for its clean, minty, fruity taste reminiscent of a Chinon.

Cave Coopérative 'Les Vignerons Réunis'
36600 Valençay

Château de Pocé.

Back in Touraine I stopped at the cooperative cellar of Francueil, a typically ugly edifice, built just around the back (shielded, thankfully, by a wood) of glorious Chenonceaux, the loveliest château of all. The *directeur* sat me at a desk in a sort of schoolroom and gave me, complete with blackboard sketches, a very thorough dissertation. I learnt, amongst other things, that Sauvignon Blanc wines always have much more flavour on rainy days! This is an established fact, apparently, caused by something to do with barometer going down? I suggest you test the theory.

The wine I plumped for is rather unusual, but it stood out clearly from the other reds by being black — or very dark red, anyway. It was a Cot, pronounced like Sebastian 'Coe'. In Bordeaux it is called Malbec and in Cahors Auxerrois. Confusing ... but interesting. The wine was obviously *le directeur's* pride and joy, and he had won a silver medal in Paris with it.

Cave Coopérative de Francueil
37150 Bléré

As I was leaving I noticed one of those old mobile distilleries steaming away at the back of the cellar. I find these *distillerries ambulantes* fascinating things. They are generally run by highly skilled, red-nosed gentlemen who travel the land with their rusty old steam engines, setting up shop wherever there is anything that can be distilled into something more usefully potent. The right of private individuals to employ these distillers was long ago officially rescinded, and now only a few persons of great age retain the privilege of being a *Bouilleur de Cru*. It is said that some families have been known to keep great granny going year after year with injections, pills, drip-feeds and so on, just so they can still claim her ration of home-made brandy!

However, that day they were working at the cooperative distilling the left-overs: the foul-smelling grapeskin and pulp residue of the wine-presses. I once had a job shovelling that stuff, its alternative use is fertilizer and it smells like it! But miracle upon miracle, if it is tipped into one of these boilers, first comes this gorgeous smell of plum jam, then after some minutes a bright stream of clear spring water. (Well it *looks* like spring water!) Do stop if ever you see one of these things by the road, they are always happy to let you sip some, still warm from the tap. Perhaps your contortions as the grenade goes off in your mouth amuse them. 'Not bad,' you wheeze, blinded by tears!

My last stop was Montlouis. Almost on the edge of Tours itself and suffering from Bungalowitis, a creeping growth that destroys vineyards. Montlouis is south across the River Loire from Vouvray. In fact its wine is often

Mobile Still – Francueil

compared unfavourably — one is forced to add — with Vouvray. This may be a mistake, for the Montlouis vines are not sited upon the disadvantaged north-facing bank of the Loire, as people tend to assume, but upon the sun-blessed south-facing banks of the River Cher, a tributary. The Berger brothers seem to be the acknowledged star performers of the region; they are certainly a pair of real hard workers. If bad weather interrupts their vineyard work they just get their chisels and go below to chip a few more metres of cellar out of the chalk! Their *caves* are all the more impressive for being home dug. They even have a cosy little tasting bar — every home should have one. Their wine goes partially into *méthode champénoise,* and then into either sec or demi-sec *nature* (still) wines of Chenin Blanc. Although the semi-sweet was much the most pungent wine, I plumped for the more discreet sec. It had the clear, soft taste of Chenin, often said to resemble the flower of acacia trees. For me the similarity was much more with quince. We had a whole bowl from our tree last year and although we did not eat them the aroma filled the house for weeks.

Messieurs Berger Fréres
Cave des Liards
Saint Martin le Beau
37270 Montlouis-sur-Loire.

—STAGE 10—
The Great
Wines of Touraine

FROM Montlouis I made a hop over the Loire to Vouvray which is possibly one of the best known wine areas to the British because of its proximity to the Great Road South (N10) at Tours (turn left at the bottom of the hill before crossing the river into Tours). Vouvray must be a very ancient dwelling place. It began as caves cut into the soft limestone of the sunny, south-facing cliff by the waters edge. And here the cave habit lingers on, even to the present day millenia after most of us moved above ground.

Vouvray remains troglodytic. Most of the town's fine house façades were built for appearance sake; but the houses themselves run back into the cliff face where the cave-rooms are indistinguishable from any others, apart from a certain lack of windows. On some of the little side ravines the less fashionable 'houses' are just caves with bright painted shutters and chimneys that poke up through the vineyards on the 'roof'. While cheap and very cosy, they do make for a lot of pleurisy!

Balzac lived in the flashiest of domiciles,

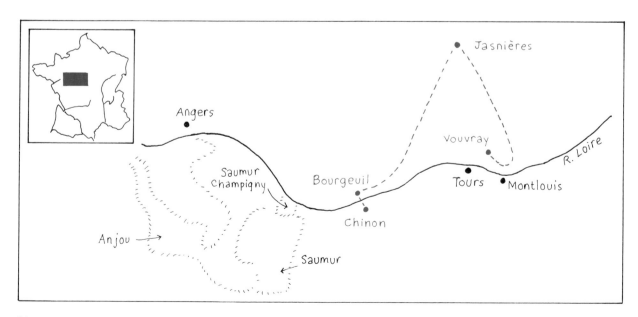

Château Moncontour
- the Grand.

Château Moncontour, a turretted splendour inhabited now by a glamorous, very Parisienne widow from whom it was my fawning, tongue-tied pleasure to buy wine in the early days. She used to receive me on the terrace by the terracotta, draped in mink and afghan hounds and wearing boots of unbelievable length. The hounds chewed my ears as I cringed on about her excellent 1967 or something equally boring. I think she may have known I was there but I am not sure. Nowadays, well, nowadays being married, with the children and all that, I have to pick my suppliers with more care. Moncontour is no more for me ... but Madame Freslier, down the road, is about right.

The large floral pinny was repeatedly smoothed with anxious flour-covered hands, 'Mais les hommes sont à la vigne!' Quel despair! The stupid English wine merchant turns up at 10.00am. The men — husband André and son Jean-Pierre — are of course away in the vineyards (five hectares up near Moncontour). She will have to take me round the cellar herself. Switching off the oven first — no tarte-aux-pommes today and very nervous and shaky with the rubber hose — she siphoned wine out of their big *tonnes* at the back of the *cave*. Between us we filled a bottle or two to take home and liberally washed down the floor in the process. *I* showed *her* how to push the bottle against the wall to drive in the cork. Obviously the divide between cellar and kitchen is

a strict one, chez Freslier. It is gorgeous stuff to taste though. Some wines are just made for tasting; and wines made from Chenin Blanc are always the most drinkable of drinks even straight from the barrel on their own. Most red wines seem to need the complement of food; the drier whites require a biscuit or peanut to placate the taste buds; and the dessert wines need well ... just their desserts. But mid-sweet, acid-sweet Vouvray, like a Mosel, needs nothing. The high acidity refreshes; the pungent quince apple-blossom aroma entertains; and the fat-butter sweetness satiates. Finally, a clean acid after-taste tidies up the palate for more! I bought the Famille Freslier's 1982 'demi-sec' — only just sweet — from the patch they call the 'Petit Fosse'.

Monsieur André Freslier
'La Caillerie'
(par la Vallée Coquette)
37210 Vouvray

I continued north to the confusing River Loir. You may note the absence of the 'e'; this is the male tributary to the north of the big, fat, female River Loire. You knew that of course but people like me — who decided long ago that the French insistence on bringing sex into everything, with all their le's and la's, was a nonsense best ignored — we find the Loir confusing. Its vineyards are a faint northern echo of the Loire's. South-facing slopes around La Chartre and east past Montoire, toward Vendôme, sprout spasmodic, rather scrappy vineyards. They make wines that with very high acidities display clearly the region's borderline climatic situation.

To digress, if you participate in the regular summer stampede south out of Le Havre, consider leaving the main Alençon, Le Mans, Tours fast-track, and instead incline eastwards on good empty roads through lovely places like Mortagne-au-Perche (world capital of black puddings!) Ferté-Bernard, La Chartre and Château Renault. (Once there, you can climb on the autoroute and by-pass Tours.) Taking this road, the first sign of wine is a little hut just north of La Chartre grandly emblazoned 'Maison du Vin-Jasnières'. It is invariably shut, but never mind. Look about you and upon the hillside you will see the first of those lovely green stripes. Proceed into the town and try Monsieur Pinon's Jasnières AOC with some nice *Moules Farcies* at the Hôtel de France. Jean-Baptiste Pinon hides himself away well, miles up river. His motto 'pour vivre heureux vivre en cachet' ('for a happy life, keep out of sight') is typical of the true French countryman, the very smart *paysan* who takes the term 'peasant' as a compliment. His Coteaux Vendomois — a *Vin Gris* in some years, in others more or less red made with the Aunis grape — is a last relic of the red grape this far north. His Jasnières is said to be very gunflinty — the burnt smell when you strike a flint — an old wine trade cliché I find hard to use because I do not go round striking flints much myself. It is as dry as a bone, or a 'leafy' white anyway.

Monsieur Jean-Baptiste Pinon
12 Promenade du Tertre
41800 Montoire sur Loire

However, Joël Gigou in La Chartre itself did have some red wine left, in the form of a nice, strangely grapefruity 1982 red. They served it at the Hôtel de France where it went down a treat with a bit of pink *Carré d'Agneau*. I must stop this drooling and get on my way.

Monsieur Joël Gigou
4 Rue des Caves
72340 La Chartre sur le Loire

I travelled down to the Loire again, west past Tours to Rabelais country. Here was a man who really knew how to get legless with some style! Chinon, Bourgueil and St-Nicolas de Bourgueil make a happy little enclave, in constant, mildly bitchy competition with each other, yet bound tight by being (with nearby Champigny) the Loire's only red wines of 'Grand Standing' (pronounced: Gron Stonding!) as the Franglais goes. In Bourgueil they will just slip into the conversation that, of course, Chinon has sold its soul by planting all those recent hectares on valley alluvium soil to churn out watery pinks for the tourists, while Bourgueil has primly kept herself to a strict coteaux-slope, classic-site position! 'With wine as tough as Bourgueil, you wouldn't expect much demand for new plantings' is Chinon's general response to that one. No matter.

Allow me to sum up the general 'house' styles of the three districts. Bourgueil is a big red, well, big for the Loire anyway. Made like the others from the Cabernet Franc grape, it can resemble a Saint Emilion claret. This quality is thanks to the tufa subsoil. The soft rock (in which they also find

Monsieur Gigou's rather unsophisticated but effective form of advertising.

it easy to tunnel their cellars) gives wines of great longevity; I tried a 1955 that evening and it was still a tannic and healthy bright red wine. (One of the characteristics, apparently, of tufa grown reds is their ability to stay ruby red and avoid browning like most.) My supplier is a young man of messianic zeal called Pierre-Jacques Druet. After training in both Burgundy and Bordeaux and ending up with impressive letters after his

name, he chose Bourgueil of all places to make his reputation. He feels he can really do something in an area fallen just a little behind the times due to those easy pickings from tourists — not that he is a modernist. A true fanatic, he insists on retaining, for example, the old oak fermenting vessels long since slung out by most of his classmates in favour of steel. Everything else is pure egg-white fining; *semi-macération*; new oak-barrel ageing; heavy old bottles; and of course the very traditional steep price. No, seriously, I think he works for love not money. However, making wine like he makes it just costs a lot.

Monsieur Pierre-Jacques Druet
La Croix-Rouge
Bénais
37140 Bourgueil

Consider Bourgueil as the hardest of the three reds and generally bigger, stonier, tougher, and closed-up when young. It could be classed as a fairly 'butch' bottle that virtually all your guests will think is claret. The key flavour to look for is violets; but if you want a challenge see if you can pick out cassis, mushrooms and Cordoba leather,

they are favourite local terms. Chinon is more feminine: soft, floral, vanilla-ish and seductively gulpable. Rabelais' tasting-note was taffeta. Thank you Rabelais. If Bourgueil can do the job of claret, then good, fresh Chinon (which is hard to find) does just what Beaujolais does. It is curious that two wines made so close and with the same grape should be so different.

I visited Bernard Baudry, a nice lad not too much a fanatic — who seems to enjoy himself. His vines are at Cravant-les-Coteaux, in the heartland of the appellation; and he, along with the rest of his brothers, cousins *et al*, fairly dominates the medal-winning league. In a small, neat, partly troglodytic cellar we 'vertically' tasted his 1982s down to a 1976 'great' year. He was keeping the 1976 for himself, but the 1982 I did rather fancy. It was a cuvée made just with fruit from old vines. 'Rich bon-bon anglais (boiled sweet), jammy' was my memorable note; it had no toughness at all. Such terms rather imply the wine is sweet which it is not, nor of course is it bone-dry. I prefer the wine in this youthful state; later on the characteristics of maturity are interesting but no more than interesting in my view — even with their bouquets of hides, leather, or bananas even!

Monsieur Bernard Baudry
Coteaux de Sonnay
37500 Chinon

Confusing the issue, St-Nicolas de Bourgueil wines which are grown on sand, are much more like Chinons than Bourgueils, often even softer in my experience. They are also thinner, but that is not necessarily pejorative. The St-Nicolas I finally found after several visits is one of the most gloriously ethereal red delights I have ever tasted — Fleurie included. We drank an awful lot of St-Nicolas that day in the name of research (all due to the fanatical Druet's desire to locate 'The Perfect Wine'). I vaguely remember talking to someone's pet marcassin (a baby wild pig), and then spending an evening rushing round some *caves* looking for the 'lost entrance to Grandfather's cellar'. Cheers!

Gaec Olivier, Bernard et Patrick
la Forcine
Saint Nicolas de Bourgueil

—STAGE 11—
Champagne

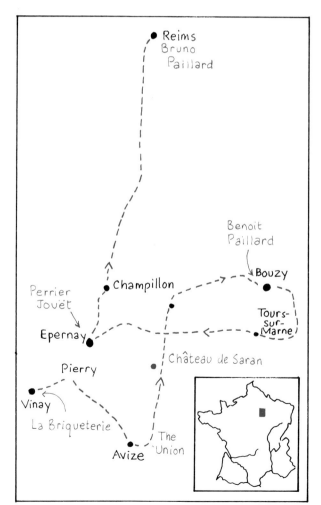

CHAMPAGNE is the handiest of vineyards from the British point of view. You can drive from anywhere in southern England in time to take a glass of that most miraculous of restoratives before dinner. It is only three or four hours drive from Calais these days, with motorway assistance, and it is a specially blessed place. It seems that it is always sunny and embarrassingly prosperous. Like a magical island Champagne is set in the bare northern French ocean of corn and sugar beet. Land in AOC Champagne is worth forty times that around it, and the Champénois complain of penury!

The land is chalk which in parts runs about 650 feet thick. Underground it is soggy and the consistency of cheddar. The chalk explains why Champagne is what it is — no chalk, no Champagne. Only on chalk do the vines produce their best and only deep down in the ground can you make wine 'prendre de mousse' or 'take the fizz'.

There is an elegance about the place although I would not say that it is a particularly beautiful region. I think the 'Montagne' of Reims is a bit of an exaggeration for a start (it is only 200 feet) and the architecture is not my style either — rich burgher stuff and 100 years old maximum, mostly. But there is an elegance in the way of life ... 'style' might be a better word.

In other wine regions growers of the horny-

Down in the real chalk cellars — the 'crayères'.

handed-sons-of-the-soil type will think nothing of jerking open a grimy bottle of their best Hermitage, Nuits or St-Emilion and dashing it into tumblers upon the green check oil-cloth kitchen table, but not here. Here, there is always a little ceremony. It is impossible to open Champagne quickly and the ritual usually includes presentation with tall flute glasses, silver tray and white napkin. Remember that no matter how Herculean the task, cork removal must always be done with composed features and an ongoing witty banter. No facial rictus and no cringing out of the line of fire, and above all no BANG! (Anyone caught banging Champagne corks is a peasant or English.) But of course, should he be a milord then it is okay. For it was the milords and their ladies who in the early days put Champagne where it is and must always remain — at the top of the social drinking tree.

Through helping to organize wine tours I discovered the Hôtel La Briqueterie just south-west of Epernay, and there I headed. It is 'twee' but very comfy, peaceful and friendly; I recommend it. The restaurant is excellent but becoming pricey, especially when you find yourself, as I did, drinking Champagne with every course and indeed on every possible occasion.

My first appointment the next day was in Avize which is capital of the white part of Champagne. The Union, which is really a wine growers' cooperative with a difference, had been good to me. As with all cooperatives the members look after their own vineyards, harvest and then take their grapes into a central cellar where the wine is made as a normal wine, without the bubbles. Then all the cellars in the Union, a dozen in all, send their grapes to headquarters to be champenized. Then three or four years later the finished wine is sent back to the individual growers in 'naked' bottles to be labelled and sold. Personally, I am not too certain of the ethics of the last bit.

Union Champagne
51190 Avize

I am only really interested in the wine that remains at the Union. I have bought it for many years and in youthful days sold lots to a big store group who were at the time more experienced in gents' underwear. Nowadays, the Union will

even stick my name on the label, which is very good for the ego. I am not pretending I make it but I do, however, select my cuvée (blend). Personally, I am dead against blends as a rule and always have been. Blended Bordeaux and Burgundy? Rubbish, and dubious authentic rubbish usually. But Champagne is the only place where I have been convinced that the blend is greater than the sum of the parts, but more on that later.

Back at the Union in the big office block complete with foyer with plant jungle, coffee tables, magazines and lifts (this is a wine cellar?) we met Michel Cestia. He is slow talking, beaming and friendly with no snappy executiveness, this *is* a wine cooperative for sure. We discuss the latest problems which turn out to be purely figurative. They may know how to make wine but their accounts are lousy. We made a long tour around the bowels of the earth (down four floors in the lift) and looked at the millions of bottles just lying there, bubbling extraordinarily slowly. The tasting room has a marvellous big dining table which seats about forty — we should all have one, although you would have to lean over a bit to get at your food because a wide steel guttering projects from under the edge all the way round. If you touch a foot pedal water streams alarmingly from the table towards your lap before being ducted away down discreetly hidden pipework.

At this point I decided to have the full range of their styles played on me. They are all blends and they are all finished here, but that is where the similarity ends. First, I tried several cuvées of their main wine, a Blanc de Blancs, through different bottle ages and different levels of sweetness. If you thought Brut meant dry, you are wrong, by the way. It means 'relatively dry'. In fact, I do not know if there is a totally, totally dry wine. This may hurt a little but the wine trade everywhere says that the customer 'talks dry but drinks sweet'. This wine was not exactly sweet but definitely off-dry with between 10 and 15 grams of sugar per litre. It is not detectable as sweetness except by a trained taster but it is there and the fruity effect it creates is discernible by all.

Then we tried their 'Brut Zero' which really is dry because no sweet liqueur was added just prior to final corking. This was as close to totally dry as you can get and has accordingly earned the reputation of being a 'smart' drink, very Paris-chic. It sandpapers the mouth and strips tooth enamel, but it is nice when it stops. Here they have had the good idea of making their 'Brut Zero' a *crémant* (that is, half the fizz of a normal Champagne and 'à mon avis' better as a food accompaniment). It is truly creamy as the name suggests which makes it easy to taste the wine below the bubbles clearly. With a piece of grilled fish this wine would be nice, but on its own at Annabel's or with Auntie and wedding cake... arrghh!

The rosé came next but they would not sell me any because all the world has gone mad for pink Champagne (you see, I said all the pink drinkers would come out of the closet one day). Then we tried their 'black wine' from the farmer members at Bouzy and Ambonnay. Though made with black grapes, the colour is in fact off-white and it is nicely acid with the texture of a cat's tongue.

Before continuing, I think we need a rough geography of Champagne. Imagine the side view of a mushroom. Just above the centre of the

crown is a dot which is Reims, one of the two Champagne capitals. At the top of the stalk is the other one, Epernay. The stalk is the Côte des Blancs where only white Chardonnay grapes are grown. It slopes down left to right and Avize is in the middle. The mushroom head is the Montagne de Reims. Vines only grow around the edges (the middle is forest) and the best grow around the right-hand side edges. Here the grapes are black, but their juice, of course, is colourless. The extreme bottom right-hand edge of the head is exceptional, being the sunniest bit of all and that

is Bouzy and Ambonnay. The rest of the bottom edge is the valley of the Marne which is a relatively less favoured bit because it is largely clay soil rather than chalk, which does not work so well. They plant Pinot Meunier here, which is usually rather flavourless, but makes a good blending wine.

After lunch I went up to Bouzy and Benoit Paillard. As I said Bouzy is one of the hottest places in Champagne, grows almost only black Pinot Noir and is therefore not too surprisingly the only place where they make a fair bit of red wine. It tastes like a severe Burgundy; it is tougher and without the ample bosom of the Côte d'Or and it also costs the earth.

Benoit and his wife run a lovely little business which is immaculately kept. The big gates open into a gravel yard with tractors, kennels and so on. It all seems very natural until you find out that they excavated the whole thing to put in the big underground car park that he calls the cellar. Now they've put the yard back, nobody knows. This sort of building job gives you a vague idea about how much money they make in Champagne. Benoit also installed a lift which takes you down first to the cellar, and then further down to the *crayères* — the real chalk cellars, 50 feet down. Down here the bottles are really snug. The rock has been cut with a knife and you can still pinch bits out with your fingers. When the still wine has been bottled with a bit of yeast and sugar to fizz it up, it sits down here for a year or two, or three, absorbing — as slowly as possible — the carbon dioxide from the imprisoned fermentation into the liquid at higher and higher pressure. Bottles are stacked in great piles and if you tripped and fell down here it could cost a fortune. Benoit's speciality, for me, is his red which is expensive but also very rare.

Pierre Paillard
51100 Bouzy

The following day I wanted to take my three travelling companions to see one of the places that made Champagne the great drink that it is (that is, to one of the great Houses — the Grands Marques). We were invited to Perrier-Jouët whose 'Palais' (terms like 'offices' or 'works' hardly seem appropriate) is fitted snugly between the Palais Moët and the Palais de Venoge on the Avenue de Champagne in Epernay. Frédérique, the appropriately sparkling daughter of the *maître de cave*, gave us the tour. First we saw the miles and miles (and ever expanding) of underground roadways on several levels. Every now and then as they dig, they burst through into a Moët (or someone else's) *gallerie*. They say that you can cross the town in secret if you know the way.

Perrier-Jouët
51201 Epernay
(Marne)

Then we went for the most fascinating of tastings with Fred's father. It was time for him to 'faire sa cuvée' and therefore a good time to call. We stood very quiet alongside the Perrier-Jouët directors as the big man set out a long row of numbered bottles of the still white wine samples of 1984's crop on the big table in the white tasting room. He then very kindly took us on what was effectively a verbal guided tour of Champagne villages explaining at length why each tasted the way it did. Cramant was lovely ripe Chardonnay from a prime site village; Chouilly was much less ripe and from a back valley; Ay near Bouzy was a lovely Pinot Noir, the wine slightly tinted by the black skins; Vertheuil, from the Val de Marne was a Pinot Meunier wine, dull and bland; Mailly in the north proved stony and tough, Vincelles a dull Meunier and Bouzy big and magnificent. He thoughtfully tipped different amounts of these wines into a tall calibrated cylinder and we tasted the result. It was better than anything so far, even the dull Meunier was playing a useful role somewhere in the *assemblage*. Then, he added his reserve wine which was a blend of older vintages kept back down in deep stone vats to give maturity, mellowness and complexity to the new. It certainly did! The result, although a plain, still and slightly cloudy wine could be identified as a proto-Champagne. The imminent second fermentation in the bottle would now add bubbles and extra flavour elements (things like complex amino acids) to make a great Champagne.

Bruno Paillard
Champagne Bruno Paillard, S.A.
rue Jacques Maritain
51100 Reims

Our last call was to have been my broker in Champagne, the now renowned Bruno Paillard. I started with his father many years ago and doubts at being handed down to the boy have since been confounded. He now spends so much time in America, Japan or wherever that he can never see me. His wines are everywhere and he now has a very modern flashy cellar of his own to play with. Mark my words he will be the first 'new' Grand Marque in Champagne in 100 years. I have already tried some of his 1975 vintage and it is gorgeous. Just another glass of the stuff before we go, shall we?

—STAGE 12—
Back to Bordeaux

I WAS driving at night down the Tours/Bordeaux section of the A10 autoroute after a spell back in Britain. It was October 3rd and the back of the car was stuffed full of wellies, macs and woolly sweaters. The rain forced us to keep the windows shut on the

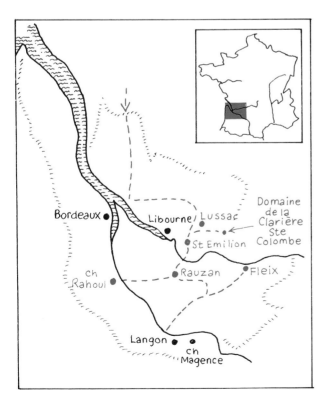

motorway but as we finally negotiated the St-André/Libourne intersection we wound down the windows. There was a magical moment as the hot night air gushed in with 'that smell'. Like Proust and his wretched 'madeleine' cakes, one sniff galvanized the cortex: it said 'wine' and 'harvest'; it said hot, bubbly, sticky, half-born wine; and it said it at its most aromatic with that black-curranty, tarry, jam making smell. It was all around us in the dark. Yet it was invisible apart from the cellar lights of the more diligent *vignerons* who were assisting the birth through the night. Big vats, open at the top, were bubbling out their aromas which blanketed the countryside in five hundred square miles of bouquet.

All the images of harvest rushed back in memories of nearly fifteen years ago. For since then dear old Bordeaux Direct has kept me moving so fast I have not actually worked a vintage. It is not the same just being the buyer from outside and passing, all too rapidly, through. There is something about being part of the vintage that is magical. The rest of the wine year is so calm and peaceful ... boring even. Then 'Bang!', with September the party is off. Hundreds more folk arrive, clanking old machinery is started up for its ten days of activity a year, and all is noise, bustle, apparent chaos, hot heat, and bright light. The only thing talked of is the wine in making ... excitedly in good years: 'on a fait 14.5° hier!', 'C'est rien ça, à

Gardegan il y avait un lot de Merlot à 17°'. They exaggerate degree strength (measured as sugar = potential alcohol) in the same way some fishermen boast of length, car buffs of acceleration. They warn each other of the multitude of dangers at this delicate birth moment: 'On m'a dit qu'il y a pas mal du 'Blackrot' à St-Emilion.' Trust the French to employ English words for something as nasty as Blackrot! There is often an element of the ceremonial. The fat burghers of St-Emilion risk cardiac arrest as, red-robed and red-faced after a good lunch, they wheeze and squeeze up to the top of the old Norman Keep (La Tour du Roi) to declare the harvest open. It is a declaration totally ignored by wine makers who start when they please. The play-safe 'chicken' types start dead early with unripe grapes; and the better, braver wine makers risk rot, mildew and diluting-rain, to hang on later for perfect ripeness.

There are parties every day on the good estates. The big harvesters' lunch at long trestle tables is more or less a party too. It is simple though and often starts with *soupe de legumes* full of whole carrots, spuds, cabbage leaves and big chunks of bread. The Spanish migrant workers chop a dried red pimento they carry in their pocket to spice up their bowl ... and set on fire the mouths of naïve, unwary British students. Everyone adds a little red wine to their last dregs and tips the bowl to their lips — a *chabrol*. The good simple fare continues with pork, beef, andouillette, big bowls of steaming petit pois, noodles, rice, frites. Finally, hunks of cheese and a raw red 'Gros-Rouge-que-tache' set the seal on the afternoon. (In Bordeaux the estate wine is too expensive to be served; instead we drank the rough, blue-red stuff bought in from the cheapo merchants.) Above all, the wine harvest is time-off from the real world. Harvest has its own problems, often considerable, but at least they and the frenzied work and socializing keep you so busy — from dawn till after midnight — there is no time for other worries. If they start World War III I hope they start at harvest time.

All that, I thought as I wound down the car window.

But there was something new this year: cartloads of grapes were moving lethally slowly on the road at night with no lights! Soon we found the reason: a huge combine-monster was whacking grapes into its skirts and hoppers right through the night. It was quicker, and allowed the

All hands are needed when gathering in the grapes.

night-cooled grapes to be picked for less tempestuous fermentations. But it does bruise and split the fruit and it certainly chases away some of that warm human feeling. It also filled the night with a humming roar as if the whole countrysid had been badly air-conditioned.

We settled into our home at Ste-Colombe feeling as if we were gate-crashing halfway through the party. The gypsies celebrating the night away had taken over. The tumbledown outbuildings next door were already shaking with the violent fermentations bubbling within.

I went first to see *La Cave* at Lussac. It is just 'the cellar' to us, for it is where we began — I washed bottles there in 1966. It is a big, ugly place which I adore. 'Monsieur' used to take me there daily in his 2CV and taught me French, sound business-theory, philosophy, and the good points of Napoleon Bonaparte, all along that winding

Château Rahoul.

four kilometres. He too needs no more name than 'Monsieur'. We still *vous* rather than *tu* but he is my French father. Jean Cassin is Bordeaux Direct's father too. If you like Bordeaux Direct you more or less have to like the immaculately made Roc. Do not knock it, as the saying goes.

Les Propriétaires Réunis
Puisseguin
33570 Lussac

The next day I made a tour round the Entre-deux-Mers wine cooperatives with Foucaud (old super-nose). He oversees about 40% of what gets made in Bordeaux as the head wine-maker of the united cooperatives. We went to see the new 1983 whites at Landerrouat, Sauveterre, Blasimon and Rausan. Dramatic changes had taken place in three years. There were a lot of keen young wine makers desperate to create glories, but all still saddled with museum-piece equipment. I wanted to pluck the best vats this year before the hordes arrive, and to wrap all their live flavour in tight, glass bottles for Christmas to avoid losing any of that fruit. We arranged a little competition for later in November to pick the best vats and try for that early bottle. This is the secret to better white wines. The cooperatives' best reds of 1982 had become splendid, muscular young beauties. What a vintage!

At Graves (Portets) we went to visit Peter, who is the one person I most want to teach me wine making. Peter Vinding-Diers not only makes wine the way I want to make it when our vineyard begins to produce, but in addition is capable of explaining just how he is doing it. There he was dressed in wellies, shorts, and a long rubber apron (very M.A.S.H.), running his hands through the entire crop. He likes to touch it all. Black magic? Laying on of hands? He insists, (as so few others do) on hand picking grapes into baskets. They are then transported unbruised and tipped onto his workbench for the master's

personal '*triage*' before crushing. He pulls all the rotten bunches out. This may not be so important in good years but it does mean he makes wine almost as good in bad years. And good wine in bad years is the sign of the 'Great Wine Maker'. The white Rahoul is already fermenting and it is doing so in new oak casks! 'Only Haut Brion does that,' you may say. Well, now it is Haut Brion and Rahoul. The smell at the bung-hole was amazing! I tasted the 1981 red and signed up to take all Peter will give to Britain every year, for as

long as he likes. When you see a really good thing, there is no point in taking half-measures; go for it 100%.

Peter Vinding-Diers
Château Rahoul
33640 Portets

Magence, further down the Graves, is the home of the ever-young bachelor boy, Dominic

The harvest arriving at the Cave de Lussac.

Guillot de Suduiraud (Giy-oh for short!) He will probably cut off supplies to me if he sees me saying he is now the grand old man of modern white wine-making in Bordeaux. But he was the first with his stainless-steel, water-cooled, CO_2-soused winery to make Sancerre-style, green-grass, Sauvignon whites. His white is the boy soprano to Peter's Maria Callas.

Château Magence
St Pierre de Mons
33210 Langon

I have been shilly-shallying about a real Saint Emilion for years now. I know them well but have always thought the 'satellite' Saint Emilions like Lussac and Puisseguin offered much better value. Now having gained a reputation for being a lad who only buys good stuff (and buys large amounts too) I have been honoured by the new 'star' of Saint Emilion approaching me to be his agent. Since young François de Ligneris took over the reins this Château Soutard has raced to the fore. Splash-decant it three hours before dinner for the best effect.

Monsieur de Ligneris
Château Soutard
33330 St Emilion

SAINT EMILION

—STAGE 13—
A Day in the Médoc

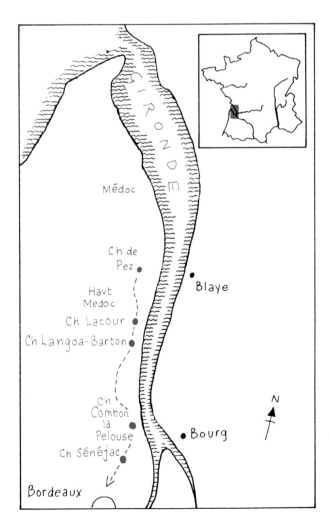

WHEN I arrived in Bordeaux the harvest was just about over. At this point the keener type of wine grower gets an urge to leave his bubbling vats and rush around quizzing his neighbours, looking at their bubbling vats, sharing a few glasses and generally letting off steam. It is rather like students going mad after exams: 'What did you think about that ghastly one on Archimedes' sort of thing. In Bordeaux it is more in the line of, 'Oh that temperature, Mon Dieu I thought it would never come down, all night we hosed,' (natter, natter) 'sparged with nitrogen then racked off 0.5 residual,' (natter, natter). Peter Vinding-Diers, in whose Graves cellar I had been studying techniques for my own baptism of wine, evinced a strong desire to go and check out his chums in the Médoc. I was invited along. This is the story of that day in late October.

Thanks to a slight contretemps with a radar trap I missed catching Peter up at Pez. Peter has a lot of time for Pez because the owner, Robert Dousson, is a real 'hands-on' farmer like himself. Big, burly and bursting with enthusiasm, he is far from one of your 'pop-down-from-Paris-for-the-harvest-if-I've-got-the-time' absentee landlords. It seemed not to matter that we were late, he good-naturedly set about repeating the tour of the cellars. What a *cuverie* they still have at Pez! And that huge battery of mammoth oak *cuves* or 'fermenters' as the Australians would say — ten

Château Latour.

feet in diameter, fifteen feet high ⬥ are only in use those few weeks in the year. The rest of the time they are a nightmare to keep clean and free from infection, I imagine. We watched them do this. Despite the fact that they expected to continue harvesting almost another week (they had had bigger crops than even the massive 1982 at the top end of the Médoc) they were washing and scrubbing down all the presses and equipment. Hygiene is crucial to good modern wine making. Cruddy old 'it'll be all right on the night' cellars are going out of fashion!

Château de Pez
St. Estèphe

As I travelled on towards Pauillac, I noted the Cos d'Estournel's pagoda façade twinkling in the morning sun on one side and huge Lafite on the other. Trundling great harvesting machines were all around. Lafite is determined to prove they can still maintain their quality by mechanical means. Even Mouton has gone part mechanical now. We'll see! We'll see! But our next call was to a place where tradition is strictly adhered to. Heaven knows how many human harvesters Latour employs, but the rest of the year the complement is 80 people — and that for just 110 acres! I glimpsed Peter turning in through those stately gates and, glad to have caught up, somewhat carelessly swerved in after him — cutting across and upsetting a choleric old boy in an ancient black auto. We rang the bell for admittance to the Great Courtyard; and I cannot remember how it happened but I suddenly found myself completely alone in the first-year *chai*! Panic seized me as I realized there was just me and thousands of gallons of the most beautiful wine in the world. What a temptation! I found the others in the vat room looking at the new born baby and talking of 'grassiness' in the press wine. Jean-Louis Mandrou — languid, elegant pin-striped wine maker (under the renowned Jean-Paul Gardère) — gave us the tour. We moved on to the second-year *chai*, a bottle cellar which was a maze of stone bins and vintages dating back to 1949. The really old stuff is kept under the château itself and dates back to 1861! They have another place with a million bottles of the new stuff elsewhere — a million bottles at £20 each!

Château de Pez.

La Tour de Latour

Château Latour
33250 Pauillac

Top wine-makers like Peter admire Latour as being technically the best of the First Growths: Latour, Lafite, Mouton, Margaux, Haut Brion. Writers and wine-lovers of the richer sort may wax lyrical about Margaux's 'seductive femininity' compared to Lafite's 'elegant silkiness'. But a lot of that is strictly for the birds. Latour is, however, as Jancis Robinson put it '... the claret man's claret!' One can actually quantify the quite extraordinary pains taken at Latour. It is wine making at a sublime level. Take for example, the eggs! Latour casks are 'racked', which means that the wine is cleaned by an inert colloidal substance; once it is tipped into the barrel it forms a slow-sinking film that nets out unwanted particles suspended in the liquid. You can get various synthetic powders for this but at Latour they still use eggs — egg whites to be precise. Six eggs a barrel, four times a year in 1,500 barrels is 36,000 egg whites. (What about the yolks? Soufflé for lunch *again*!) Well all right that is just a tradition and others do the same. But where others follow blindly, Gardère and Co. really think. Most other châteaux whisk the whites; Latour does not, thus conserving intact the long microscopic filaments that really do the trick. That is tradition *and* modern know-how!

Now, I accept that I often go 'over the top' with my wine descriptions. I am unrepentant, but it does leave me stuck when trying to describe the wine we tasted that morning — the 1981 Latour. 'Black and dark' I scribbled (confused aleady); I continued with 'Berryfruit Cabernet, mint, eucalyptus, various herbs and warm, wet oak'; and concluded with 'it all lasts an age'. I eventually decided to buy the châteaux's 'second' wine, Les Forts de Latour, which is made from the younger vines. The impact of such wine can stun you! I was taken away in a daze (like Toad going 'poop-poop...') for lunch with 'Uncle Ronald'. Ronald Barton, doyen of that great

After the pause Peter's wife Suzy melted 'Uncle Ronald's' freezing look and I was able to enter the portals of Château Barton, diminished but still alive. We toured the *chais*. Ronald is of the 'old school' and they know their business backwards, do the Bartons. We repaired to La Savoie in St-Julien. In spite of the unprepossessing exterior it provides an oasis in the gastronomic desert of the Médoc. Mr Barton was not over-keen on nouvelle cuisine sized portions (know the old 'NC' joke: 'And how did you find your meat, sir?' 'Well, I just lifted this piece of lettuce and there it was!') but the *Chausson d'Ecrevisses en Laitue* that day was worthy of a big detour.

Château Langoa-Barton
St Julien-Beychevelle
33250 Pauillac

Sénéjac

Irish/Bordeaux family of Barton & Guestier and the great Third Growth Langoa and Second Growth Leoville estates is to English speakers, without doubt, the Grand Old Man of Bordeaux. The château is the same for both estates, and the cellars too, although the vineyards *are* different!

We hammered at the great door up on the terrace with its lemon trees. Ronald who was alone in the vast place arrived eventually. He was just recovering, he said, from some young fool carving him up at the gates of Latour! Despite my new impressive girth I cannot quite block out from view a whole Range Rover, but I tried.

We allowed ourselves a short stop at the ravishingly pretty Château Palmer, before moving on to Sénéjac. Here we visited the home of Monsieur Le Comte de Guigné, at Le Pian. 'Hi, Comte!' (He's American). Charles de Guigné comes from a great Cognac family who moved to the United States but still hold interests in France. To wit the ambling old Sénéjac. It is run now by a young New Zealand girl, Jenny Bailey, who is a wine maker of genius. She had not only been making great improvements to an already acclaimed red, but with no proper equipment she had been making a white wine that

I tasted for a laugh, then rapidly decided I had to acquire in totality.

Château Sénéjac
Le Pian Médoc
33290 Blanquefort

Night was falling and we were looking for Cambon La Pelouse. The château is one thing but the winery is what counts. We saw its stark concrete shape in the dusk, lit and still humming. One of the most modern installations in Bordeaux, it is run by one of the eighteen children of the owner! Old man Carrere's place is at Monbazillac but he owns estates in Saint Emilion and the Médoc and puts in the offspring to run them. Often half-jokingly referred to as the 'damned Carrere cooperative' they are an unstoppable family with the most down-to-earth, no-frills approach to wine imaginable. The winery is like an aircraft hangar with twenty big stainless steel vats down each side tilted diagonally on raised platforms. The fermentation is perfectly normal but when it is finished, they run off the liquid then open the big trapdoor. Whoosh! all the marc falls straight into the press. One man, five seconds, (instead of two men and three hours!) Everything is this way; the Cambon winery is the same size as Latour but employs four instead of eighty! If you are not too worried about the frills, the Cambon, immaculately made by Jean-Marc Carrere, has got to be the best bargain of the Médoc.

Château Cambon La Pelouse
Macau
33460 Margaux

Immaculate Médoc barrel-hall.

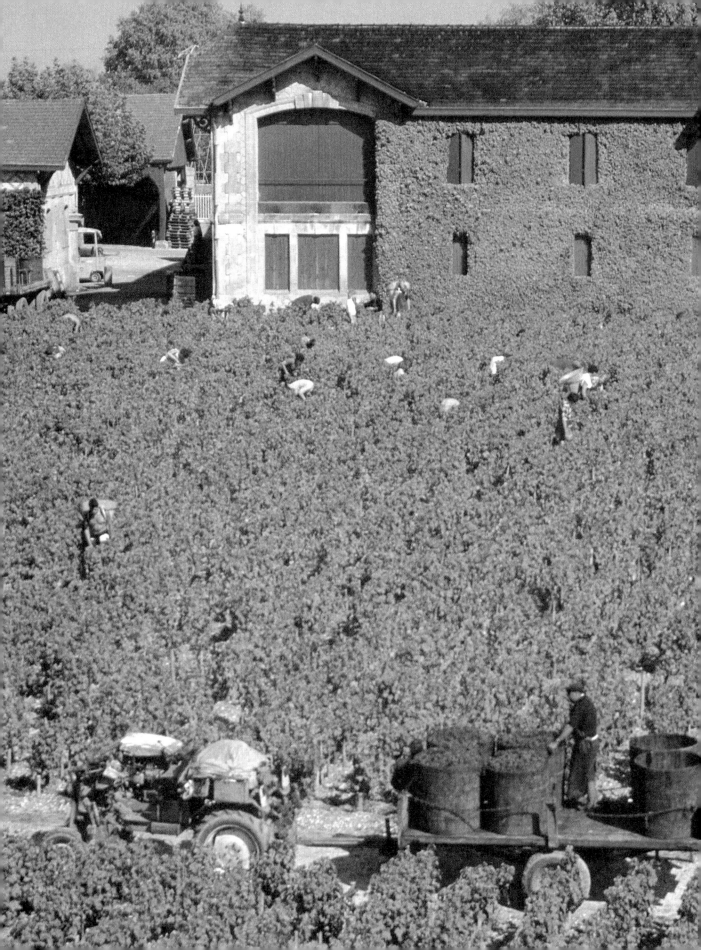

Time to get in the grapes at Château Pontet-Canet

—STAGE 14—
Gascony

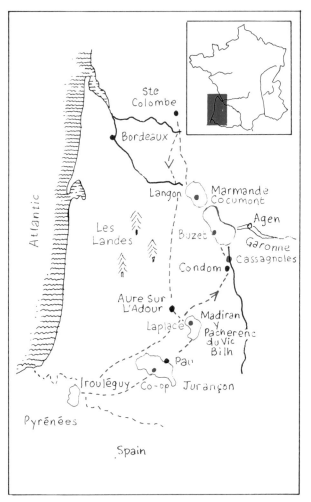

FROM Domaine La Clariere it took me from 8.00am till just before noon to reach the Gascony vineyards. Admittedly, a large chunk of this time was spent within about five miles of our goal frantically asking deaf, old Gascons 'Où est le Madiran?' This just about sums up the Gascon wine regions. They are so tiny they are easy to lose! In fact they almost did lose them. It may be a bit cruel to say so, but the most amazing thing about them is that they are still there at all. Flourishing in the Middle Ages, the vineyards of this area dwindled away to nothing when the port of Bordeaux established her stranglehold on trade. The phylloxera plague then administered the coup-de-grace.

I had crossed the Dordogne, then the Garonne, and two miles south of Langon the Bordeaux vineyards ceased and I entered the Landes. It is the largest forest in Europe outside Scandinavia: mile upon mile of dead straight pine trees with the odd isolated smallholding. These low, wooden barn-houses with their traditional big front porches were festooned with drying onions, corn cobs and such-like. Overfed geese with incipient liver problems staggered about. Timber yards and paper mills polluted the air. I once played an away match for a Bordeaux rugby team here which was abandoned when the fervent local supporters led by an infuriated, umbrella-wielding mother invaded the pitch. Arrow-straight roads allow you to drive fast through Les

Landes which I, for one, appreciate.

At Aire, on the edge of the Bas Armagnac district, one enters Béarn and the Madiran wine district ... I think. I usually get lost here! The rolling bosky hills are not unlike the Chilterns at home. It may be this apparent Englishness, the general neatness of the area, and the relative absence of advertising signs, that make me feel so at home, even though I rarely come here. It is not such a warm-country landscape as Bordeaux to the north, it seems much greener and cooler. The vineyards really have multiplied in the ten years or so since I first came. At the local cooperative in Crouseilles — when I finally found it — I discovered they were bursting at the seams with three years' excess stock. I was given a comprehensive tasting by Jean-Marc Poincot the young manager, then bundled off to the plush Ripa-Alta at Plaisance to gorge on fresh *foie gras*, freshwater prawns in sauce, and rare *magret de canard*. They are certainly keen to sell their Madiran — I even had Madiran laced with Mandarine as the house aperitif!

Cellier du Roy Henri
B.P. 9
64350 Lembeye

I went on to see the Laplace family who run the top estate in the region. At the cooperative they advised, 'You 'ave Laplace at Madiran and Triguedina at Cahors, bien sûr, 'oo else?' The Laplaces are now very big and successful but all three generations were out in the yard this bitter, spring day, all hands to the job, preparing a rush order.

Domaine Laplace
Aydie
64330 Garlin

They were glad to see me but there was some awkwardness. Grandson François was pushed forward; it had been his idea, they eventually confessed, to sell to another UK importer as well as me. They knew I would get upset, because I get very possessive about 'my' suppliers. 'But we've learnt our lesson,' they added hastily, 'l'argent est resté là-bas' ... he didn't get paid. Divine providence was on our side, perhaps? Anyway all was well with the family and me once again. I tasted two smashing vintages of their Madiran, which the Laplaces make with a higher than usual proportion of Cabernet grapes for a smoother result. Then there was an unexpected bonus. To be frank I had previously felt that the principal attribute of the region's dry white appellation, Pacherenc du Vic Bilh, was its picturesque old name. It is a very rare but generally unexciting wine made from the outlandish Rouffiac, Manseng and Courbu grapes. However, this year, the grandson in charge of the wine making, young Jean-Pierre, had really produced a blinder. Those rare old regional varietals fermented the new way (cold and slow) had produced a unique wine. Fat, rich and pungent with aromas of fruits and wild flowers, it is a winner. One sample bottle, drawn raw from the vat, stood the rough journey home and over a week half-empty in the bottom of my fridge (accidentally). I am just finishing it now as I write and it is lovely.

I was winding south down the little lanes towards Pau; all of a sudden the Pyrénées materialized through the clouds, gleaming white and ridiculously beautiful. Pau has, or rather had, great English connections. Vast Victorian villas in big gardens line the avenues. It seems that 100 years ago your wealthy Briton came here

A street scene in Bergerac.

Because of evaporation, the barrels must be regularly topped-up.

rather than Cannes or St-Tropez for his winter break. Good hunting, casinos, mountain air and Jurançon were already there and it seems we brought our golf courses and rugby football with us. But let us concentrate on Jurançon. It was renowned as the favourite tipple of great King Henry IV (French IVth) who was baptized in the stuff before he grew up, went courting and encountered the Burgundian wine of Givry, as previously mentioned. It must have gone down a bomb with those nineteenth century British, too, providing them with a sweet and luscious mid-afternoon restorative (nice with a few biscuits). Lately they have dried it out a bit to follow current trends, but on the whole the result is not successful. However, the local cooperative at Gan in the Pau suburbs, which now makes most Jurançon, does have a 'top-of-the-range' dry white wine which is outstanding by any criteria. Weighty, complex, with a bit of bottle age, it is

unlike any other wine I know. There are hints of juniper berry and honey, but it could be said to resemble vaguely a white burgundy. It is called Peyre d'Or. I have forgotten what that means but it is made from the unique local Manseng grape. The Jurançon vineyards are among the loveliest in the world. They are scattered across the steep south-facing slopes, often most attractively terraced in horseshoe form. Strung high to avoid frost, they all looked magnificent with those gleaming Pyrénéan peaks behind them. The mountains send down frost, but the occasional palm-tree alongside the vineyards reminds you just how far south you really are.

La Cave de Jurançon
64290 Gan

Irouléguy is another two hours away; it is as far south as you can go and still be in France, tucked right in under the mountains and in what is really another country. For this is Basque country and nothing to do with Béarn, Gascony or even France for that matter. Basque houses are big, white and shallow-roofed with big, open, double-storey front porches. Basque road-signs, Basque food, Basque language … and Basque wine took over. The latter is a bit of a curiosity really. Drunk locally or exported to Basque expatriates around the world, it is a light red — or rosé — made from Manseng and Courbu grapes. The cooperative, beside the road that winds up the mountains and over into another — and rather more fraught — Basque country, is just a large shed. Over the road you can watch them playing *Pelote Basque* which is a game like 'long-range' squash; played with a basket strapped to the wrist.

Cave Vinicole
Irouléguy

I drove back towards Bordeaux on a more easterly track, through Eauze, Condom and the high, open, rolling country of Armagnac to see a 'new' wine grower.

Cooperage at Buzet.

Gilles Baumann is an expatriate Alsatian married to a local girl. He makes Armagnac, and makes it very well, but his forté is a crisp, delicious (I thought it was a Sauvignon Blanc at first), dry white Colombard which has the considerable advantage of being nice and cheap mainly because it is unknown. Colombard is a grape used for Armagnac or Cognac. The French thought nothing of it as a wine grape until some of them tasted what it was made into in California and had a rapid re-think. Good Colombards are now appearing but Baumann's is the best I have tried. One unique advantage he has over other regions is that he does not have to press his grapes. He can afford to take just the best part of the grape leaving the 'free run' juice, as the inferior press-wine goes automatically for distilling. After that his secret may be he is always clean, tidy, careful and meticulous (unlike most southern French) and the result, I believe, is a top quality French white.

Gilles Baumann
Domaine des Cassagnoles
32330 Gondrin

Buzet is a wine region on the Garonne which did in fact die away completely, to be rebuilt from scratch. There is now a modern cooperative and I think no more than two independent estates. The cooperative has its own cooperage and a clever compressed air system for simplifying the huge labour of barrel-ageing. The wine is essentially claret-by-another-name, and a cousin to Bergerac AOC. But their systems make it affordable to drink their oak-aged Cuvée Napoléon for way less than a comparably finished Bordeaux.

Cave des Côtes de Buzet
Buzet sur Baize
47160 Damazan

The next door neighbour of Buzet is the Marmandais, centred around, not too surprisingly, Marmande. They also make a good pseudo-claret but their star turn, in my view, is their white. (They would, after-all, be in Graves were it not for a most inconvenient *département* boundary.)

Cave de Cocumont
Cocumont

—STAGE 15—
The Midi II

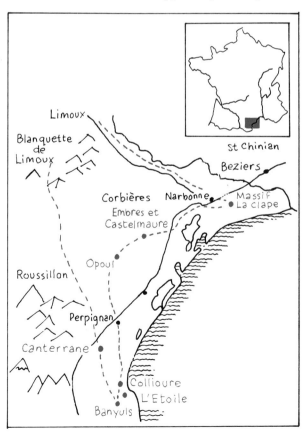

FROM Gascony I drove through the evening, down the new motorway to Narbonne to look at the southern half of the Midi. Whenever I visit this supposedly arid part of France the heavens open. This has been happening to me for twelve years now and this occasion was no different. I have hardly ever seen sunshine in the Midi. Wise old Midi growers looking up at the gathering blackness, nod their heads, draw their coats tight around them and intone 'Ah c'est Tony qui viens.' Well at least Demolombe does. He finds it hilarious — and also very useful perched up on his dry bit of rock at Pech Redon. It must have saved him a fortune in well digging. I usually stay with Demolombe these days in one of his little holiday cottages. The magic of early morning walks through the thyme, rosemary and all manner of pungent herbal smells, along the rocky heights above the Med, tempts me away from my all-time favourite hotel the 'Résidence' in the heart of old Narbonne. We ate Raclette round his kitchen table and discussed the next two days' journeyings with Andrée Ferrandiz, a lovely lady who looks after my affairs in the Midi. It is she who collects my samples, arranges my tastings, advises, then supervises bottling and despatch.

Even Andrée, however, got lost leading us to Opoul the following morning. Opoul is a typical village of the high country; nothing special just remote, poor and lovely. It happens to be in Roussillon, but only just. And many of the farms, which average a dozen or more plots dispersed all around the neighbourhood, make Corbières as well as Roussillon. This is Catalan-speaking

France, linked historically with the Barcelona/ Tarragona region south of the Pyrénées whence we get our Terra Baixa. They have a little Vin de Pays, the Côtes Catalan, and they make a couple of fortified wines: a superb Muscat de Rivesaltes to rival Beaumes de Venise, and a Rivesaltes Grenache, very like good, young, port.

In the offices of the Opoul cooperative we tasted 20 or so wines covering this full range with the *Directeur,* Monsieur Coubris. Finally I plumped for an outstandingly attractive 1983 Roussillon 100% *macération carbonique;* it was dry and black/purple (though typically such a wine sheds much of this colour in May/June). Sure enough it is now dark cherry red but it retains the attractive wild blackberry aromas that drew us all to it.

Les Vignerons d'Opoul
Opoul Perillos
66600 Rivesaltes

As we drove further south the Pyrénées broke through the cloud to hang, jewel-like, in the air, much as they had done some time before when we were at Jurançon, looking at their western end. We went up and down the Agly valley through Cases de Pène, Baixas, Estagel, Maury and so on. Further south we went to the vast estate of Canterrane and visited its no less imposing owner Monsieur Maurice Conte. Monsieur Conte made a fortune in Latin America, and having no children, now lavishes his love and dollars upon

Vineyards at Canterrane — below, and Collioure — right.

his wine. Like a fond father he does not like to see them leave home until he judges them capable of showing up to their best. So he keeps them. In fact he has two million bottles sitting underneath his house! Two million in vast underground and air-conditioned vaults. This is the place to be when the big bang comes, I can tell you. He has well over two hundred acres producing all this stuff, vast halls of vats in which to make it and then his own Aladdin's cave bit underneath. He runs it with a *caviste,* a secretary, and a computer. Monsieur Conte was much influenced by his

friends, the Calvet family, in his thinking and he is quite clear about his marketing strategy. Great Roussillon is not his aim. He wants to make a wine for all the poor souls (and there are many) who used to enjoy good, well-aged claret from petits-châteaux but who can no longer afford it. For them claret from Bordeaux is now either too young or too expensive, and often both. Monsieur Conte wants to supply them with a seven year old wine that has been sitting for at least four years in bottle and is, frankly, hard to tell from good petit-château claret. In Narbonne shops it was selling

Canterrane – Roussillon – most of its underground!

for 24F; I have a hunch it could prove hugely popular.

Monsieur Maurice Conte
Domaine de Canterrane
Trouillas 66300

I returned southward and pressed on through Perpignan down to France's southernmost wine areas: Collioure and Banyuls. They are in more or less the same area but Collioure is straight red wine, whilst Banyuls is fortified dessert wine. They huddle close between the sea-washed feet of the Pyrénées and form a bit of a *cul-de-sac* as the main road to Spain lies well inland. A very special micro climate encourages both lemon trees and strong wines. Both parts are beautiful and though stuffed to the gills with painters and sculptors, they remain living towns and are so far relatively free of the trendy ghastliness that has suffocated most of the native life of the Côte d'Azur. If you visit, be sure to take a drive up into the vineyards that hang above the towns like a Grand Circle Balcony. Nobody much lives up there and the actual wineries are in the towns themselves. We visited two: Mas Blanc has an international renown amongst the few who have heard of these wines but it is sensationally expensive. The little Etoile cooperative, however — made up of just 30 families — is more reasonable. Nonetheless these wines, given their tiny production, high costs and the thirsty tourist trade on their doorstep, are never going to be cheap. The Collioure 1982 we tried smelled of aromatic wood (though not aged in wood), of *myrtille* (bilberry), and maybe even of sea, pine and *garrigue* (that herbal Midi

Banyuls, from the terraces

98

scrubland). Remember that the grape is known to capture aromas from the surrounding air on its *pruine* (waxy surface). So perhaps I do not always imagine things. It is a big wine and heavier and more concentrated than most Midis. When you look at those poor old vines, baked on their scorching terraces (not only by the sun but also by its reflection off the water) you see why.

Société Coopérative Agricole 'L'Etoile'
Banyuls-sur-Mer 66650

Limoux is far inland. It is about here that the climate changes from Mediterranean to Atlantic. It is cooler up here and open to the winds not far from Carcassonne. Limoux, although it grows increasingly fine red wines with lots of Cabernet, is principally known for its fizz and its carnival. The two may not be unconnected as Blanquette is essentially a party wine and their carnival is one hell of a party. Blanquette is known as 'The Champagne of the South' and they would undoubtedly call it so were it not for the fact that they would certainly be taken to the cleaners by Champagne's solicitors. I cannot claim to have seen it this time around, but if you want to say an early goodbye to winter, Limoux is the place to go if Rio is out of your price range. The fizz does claim to be the oldest in the world, pre-dating Champagne by centuries. However, in the early days it was not as we know it now. It probably did fizz a bit, but only in barrels, which must have been a risky business. It seems that if you filter fermenting young wine through layers of cloth you remove the yeasts and the fermenting almost stops. If you then keep it cool, the fizzing will keep going gently all winter and spring. This was Blanquette, sweet in November, and pretty dry by June, I should imagine. Now it is made according to the Champagne method, by a huge cooperative and several independents. In style it is more austere than northern sparklers and consequently a good bet for those who go in for Brut de Brut ('zero dosage' and all that).

Cave Coopérative Blanquette de Limoux
Limoux

The last call on this little tour was Embres. Embres-et-Castelmaure to be precise which are two little villages at the head of the Vallée du Paradis. Pretty it is indeed, they tell me ... when

Ruined chapel in vineyards in Paradis gorge near Embres.

the rain stops. As I struggled to keep the drops off my camera lens and record a misty grey outline, with impeccable timing they told me that it was the first rain for six months! No, no, I am assured that those little villages, and their clever little cooperative which makes our Cuvée la Clarière white, spend most of their time under relentless meridional sunshine. It also makes a superb Corbières, the fattest, juiciest and fruitiest I have had for many a year. We returned home to dry out, after a fascinating two days and an even more fascinating selection of wines at the sort of painless price we have come to expect from the Midi.

Société Coopérative Agricole de Vinification
Embres-et-Castelmaure 11360

—STAGE 16—
Provence

YOU know how it is said that the whole world's population can stand on the Isle of Wight as long as they all stand still? Well, the event was obviously cancelled, but I am sure it is now re-staged annually on the Côte d'Azur. The overcrowding! The overheating! It does not help the wine industry much. New villas sprout up in old vineyards, and somehow people seem to care much less about the quality of wine they drink in these exotic surroundings. As a result Provence wine is often very boring, so-so stuff. It is the classic wine which is drunk initially under a romantic beach-side sunset; then deemed not to have travelled well after the second bottle fails to work the same magic when opened one wet winter evening in Wigan. In fact, the wine in the bottle has not changed at all, but the consumer certainly has! So a professional buyer must exercise great caution in this area. Wine here is a theatrical experience and a romance, rather than an alimentary liquid.

I went from Aix to the Italian border, picking up nice examples of all those incredibly rare, microscopic Provençal appellations. Some are about as common as the unicorn and just as expensive. First there were those you use to impress the boss then others were simply pure, innocent, wild-country rosés. Aix is interesting wine-wise because it is so similar to (some say better than) the Southern Rhône. Also while not at all a new region it has been 're-born' recently and possesses much more than the usual quota of

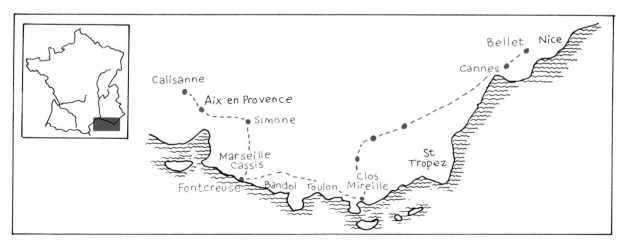

large, progressive estates owned by talented ambitious men. It is certainly far more dynamic than the rest of Provence. I met one such ambitious man who commuted to Paris in his own jet and regularly had Mitterand over for drinks! But for some time my pet estate there has been Calissanne. It used to be a haunt of the Knights of Malta but is now owned by a faceless outfit who leave Monsieur Grandchamps to run it. It is in the lower part of the district, which is much hotter than the upper zone and never has frosts. This used to mean low-acid, hot reds with a short lifespan; but new plantings of 'stiffening' varieties of grape like Cabernet, Mourvèdre and Syrah make a much more interesting wine that is carefully aged in barrels. (I noticed incidentally that they got these second-hand from Mouton Rothschild!) The 1981 was a dark, exotically fruity red, which had been softened very noticeably by its stint in the Mouton barrels.

Monsieur Grandchamps
Château de Calissanne
SCA La Durançole
13680 Lançon

South of Aix I came upon the first rarity: Palette AOC (which is a one estate AOC really). Château Simône can be glimpsed from the autoroute but is nonetheless hard to get to. Picture it as a classic little château with lawns, turrets and guided tours. Through the kitchen a door leads into solid rock and *les caves*. The machinery must have looked astonishingly new and modern in 1930 and it still functions immaculately now. They make a red, a white and even a rosé. I liked the red best with its sort of 'grand-old-claret' style. The motorway to the south then leads to the Riviera proper — or improper perhaps these days. It winds and climbs up the Massif de la Sainte Baume then at the summit the sea appears. To the left Bandol, to the right, way below, Cassis. With nothing to do with blackcurrants or anything, Cassis is a much

Château Fontcreuse.

Clos Mireille Paradise by the sea.

tarted-up fishing village, not as international as some but specializing in rest and recuperation for the tired gangsters of next-door Marseilles.

Cassis is worth a stop, especially as from the high autoroute you almost literally 'drop in' on the village. Before you do, though, you pass Fontcreuse and you should not overlook Monsieur Maffei's wine. I still have not met Monsieur Maffei though I must confess to having arrived too late for our appointment. The cellars were shut and the little château, a rather ornate villa, was tightly shuttered. Although the cellars looked well tended, the château itself had a decayed air. The garden was on a bit of a rampage, the pool was empty and the paint was peeling. *La famille* had gone away now. It struck me that it would make a good atmosphere for a French novel: a 'Farewell to France' sort of thing. I reasoned that somewhere, there would be the faithful, toothless, black-dressed old retainer. I knocked on some likely looking shutters. They did not open but there was some rather wheezy old woofing and then, on cue, a cracked crone's voice screamed, 'We're shut; monsieur's gone; fed up of waiting; go away.' This was all good, traditional French wine marketing stuff. I cannot resist that approach. I bought the white wine by telex two days later!

Monsieur Joseph Maffei
Château Fontcreuse
13260 Cassis

Over the hill, in the next bay is Bandol. I have stayed there a few times whilst leading wine-tours, and I quite like it. I especially like the Hôtel de l'Ile Rousse. A small place, immaculately run and not too unreasonably priced. There are quite a number of wine-estates for such a tiny region but then they have this vast, ever changing and wealthy holiday clientèle, so wine is good business here. The leading estate, the oldest and most quoted is Domaine Tempier.

Inland a way, beneath the rock-perched village of Le Castellet, up a long *allée* of olive trees, lies this modest domaine with its huge barrel hall. It is large, lofty and inspirational — rather like some kind of chapel, which I think it once was. Monsieur Peyraud belongs to André Roux's (Château du Trignon) small band of vine-swapping wine makers. So I knew he would be one of the obsessed. Their wine is solid stuff due to Mourvèdre, the local Bandol grape which is now being grown with success in many other hot-climate wine areas around the world.

Monsieur Peyraud Lucien et Fils
Domaine Tempier
Le Plan du Castellet
83330 Le Beausset

From Bandol I had a short drive through Toulon and along the coast to a place which is, for me, magical. Clos Mireille is an estate by the sea and when I say 'by the sea' I mean within 30

A picnic chez les Ott.

yards of the beach. That is not all; the area, the estate, and as far as the eye can see around it, is unspoilt countryside. It is probably the last such land on the whole coastline. Many, many years ago I took a course on wine at Bordeaux University. It was nothing very high-powered and the lessons on theory were much less fun than the tastings. So I drifted, as one does, to the back row and met a gangling dissolute youth from Provence by the name of Ott. Remy Ott and I became good friends but I had no idea just what his home was. It turned out that the Ott family own the largest vine holdings in Provence — three major estates and a head-office — each run by one of the four sons of the founder, Marcel Ott. They are a remarkable family and years ahead of other Provençal growers. They had impressive machinery (which they built and maintained themselves as they were good engineers) to tackle this hostile and rugged terrain. On one estate Remy showed me their *concasseur,* an iron-beast that ate up the dynamited rock fine enough to make soil fit to plant vines. They are wealthy, of

course, and their wine (mostly rosé) is easily the most expensive on the *Côte* and, at the same time, probably the best known. You see the distinctive Ott bottles poking out of ice buckets in all the best places.

Clos Mireille is their 'white' estate run by brother Henri. He grows the Ugni Blanc and Semillon grape that both do so well in the similarly hot vineyards of Australia. We climbed aboard Henri's old Citroen and he bounced me around the extensive estate. He was planting a new vineyard, using a theodolite — the Otts always do everything perfectly. Space for the vineyards had been cut out of the natural woodland which was made up of pine, cork-oak, broom and aromatic herbs. The vines are useful firebreaks against that great enemy of this paradise. The cellar has a well-watered grass roof to keep it cool. We went into the beautiful barrel hall with its shiny brass and polished wood and tried the 1983 and the 1982. I detected hints of the sea, iodine, turpentine and eucalyptus trees; it is basically a very classy number, steely, tough, big and white. As the unusual label suggests it is very expensive, but just try it — then visit the estate. After a tasting, wander, as I did in a not-too-hot May sunshine, down the track to the beach. Butterflies, buzzing insects and the distant hum of a tractor will be your only companions. Soon you see white sands, a wooded bay and not a building in sight: a perfect tropical island scene.

Société Vinicole des Domaines Ott
22 Bd. d'Aiguillon
06601 Antibes

I digress ... soon I left the coast and went inland to the valley where most Provençal wine is made. This countryside, with its bright red soils, black vines, dusting of young leaves and dramatic vineyard views is the home of Provence rosé. I went to the Union of Cooperatives. In accordance with the fashion these village-sized organizations have now grouped into a big 'macro co-op' large enough to maintain marketing departments, big flash offices, and innumerable secretaries. In other words the wine now costs more. However, they will insist that it is progress! I tried lots of pink wines and in the end could not persuade myself to pay a lot more for Rosé de Provence, a high strength wine in funny bottles, when I could get just as good in normal bottles as Vin de Pays for much less. High strength rosé is somehow fine in blistering heat, but a wine of 'normal' alcohol level is perhaps easier to take (and less dangerous) under a British sun.

Uvivar
Cave de Brignoles
83170 Brignoles

The last vineyard of France is, after a long drive east, at Bellet. I was amongst the vineyards of the municipality of Nice, a wine area so small you can easily miss it. The maps will not help you either and the locals always turn out to be visitors! Monsieur Gomez is the second largest Bellet grower with just 1.6 hectares! There are only 65 hectares in the AOC. He makes 10,000 bottles of red, white and rosé. I loved his white which was made of Chardonnay and the mysterious local Rolle. The poor soil (heavy gravel) and steep slopes rarely produce more than 35 hectolitres per hectare, only half the Bordeaux average. The 1983 white was heavy and suggested hints of broom and raspberry. Unfortunately, I could only get forty dozen; it had all been snapped up locally. I worry about Monsieur Gomez with his vineyards perched dramatically above Nice and his nice white villa with lemon trees all round. He is getting on now, and, with no heirs, was thinking he'd soon have to sell. I fancy he could be killed in the rush!

Domaine Gomez
Saint Roman de Bellet
06200 Nice

Monsieur René Gomes — Clos St. Vincent Bellet

—STAGE 17—
Savoie

SAVOIE is the French part of the Alps. It has some minute wine regions dotted about on any well sheltered slope which at not too high an altitude faces the sun. I tried to hold true to my Trek motto ('See all, drink all') by checking them all out but failed — they were very tiny and besides mountains kept getting in the way. Furthermore, some regions were definitely more mythology than fact. But in spite of all this, I found seven lovely spring-like, clean, dry whites and two reds which I could not resist.

I came back from Italy through the Fréjus tunnel. The valley from the tunnel is deeply cut, steep sided and bereft, for the most part, of either sun or mountain views. There are supposed to be vines even here, right up in the heart of the mountains, but I did not see any. Mind you, I was driving ... and it was a winding road! Once through Albertville vineyards appeared on the north bank of the Isère. First I saw a huge steep rock face which was quite bare and then I noticed the vines on the much gentler slopes right at the base. There was not much terracing and really very few vines. In fact, I have seen individual Bordeaux estates bigger than the whole lot. Yet this is the main wine producing area of the region where several villages have the right to put 'Appellation Vin de Savoie' on their label.

At one point there is a gap where a tributary runs north up to Chambéry and breaks through the mountain wall. On the other side of the gap

leadership of Monsieur Dupraz. I took the rather steep track which leads up through the woods above Apremont to a collection of wooden buildings, otherwise known as Le Vigneron Savoyard. Here I came across my first log-cabin tasting room. The people were very straightforward and friendly and they always offer you a glass of wine or six. I suspect they are glad of the company. This time they told me about their big plans to 'go stainless steel' next year. This was in an attempt to get their wines even fresher! As it is their Apremont and Abymes always make me think of snowy peaks, Alpine meadows, pretty little flowers and Heidi.

Monsieur Dupraz
Le Vigneron Savoyard
Apremont
73190 Challes-les-Eaux

The Savoyards were good enough to point me in the direction of another small, rival cooperative over the valley at Montmeillan who do the other villages' wines. I approached by way of a wandering drive through the boulders of Abymes. This is curious country — the 6,342 feet peak of Mont Granier which towers over Abymes strikes me as distinctly odd. In the year 1248 (apparently also a year of very serious flooding in Britain) half the thing fell down one night into the valley. The bits are still there, scattered about and the size of houses — tower blocks even. There is definitely something Lilliputian about Abymes with its houses and vineyards sitting amidst giant boulders.

Monsieur Louis Excoffon
Cave de Montmeillan - Coopérative des Vins
Fins de Savoie
73800 Montmeillan

At Montmeillan I found Louis Excoffon among his vats. He looked tired, as I was told he would. Fermentations were just ending (this being November) and Louis runs the co-op in such a painstaking way it was no wonder that he looked tired. He ships in all his members' unfermented musts to his central winery and makes every wine individually ... alone. He is obviously not a good delegator! I loved his Chignin, a stone-dry, low acid, classy white and similarly loved his Vin de Pays (called by the

are Apremont and Abymes. I poked around a bit trying to find out if the wines this side really were different and came to the conclusion that they were not. Chignin seems to produce the softest, least acidic wines, probably because it is quite a sun-trap. And while the local villagers have lots of fun vaunting their own and decrying their neighbours' wines as they have for hundreds of years, I find it hard to believe that even a local expert could differentiate accurately.

Differences are much more marked when it comes to grape types. The Jacquère grape is most common for white wines and there is also a fair amount of Chardonnay grown now, reflecting the Burgundian influence. The books say that the Roussette is grown here also but the books are wrong, it is grown much further north. For reds there is the unique Mondeuse grape which shows a distinct resemblance to the Syrah in style, that is cheeky, closed up, dark and with a strong bass line. They grow Gamay, too, which is not great and some Pinot Noir which conversely can be excellent. Pinot is a grape which I feel can afford to be made very light; even with little colour it is still seductive.

My suppliers in Savoie are a brave little band of eight growers, a sort of cooperative, under the

Abymes.

catchy little name of Allobroglie). But his 'pièce-de-whatsit' was his Roussette from Jongieux which is further north, up by the Lac de Bourget. I wondered if it was related to Roussanne of Châteauneuf blanc fame, because it makes a similar, broad-based, slow, majestic, grey-white wine with a subtle melon/apple taste. I tried other rarities like Bergeron and Altesse but frankly, I did not find them as delicious as the Roussette.

I stayed in Chambéry, which a lot of people believe is the centre of production of the dry vermouth industry. Well, this is another myth to explode, because it is not. They do not, surprisingly, make Chambéry in Chambéry. And it seems that nobody in Chambéry knows where they do make it, and most do not even know that there is such a thing! I first went there about ten years ago looking for the true, 'authentic stuff'. I met a bloke in an office who offered to sell me some, yet he became increasingly vague on the subject of where it is made. I ended up on a trading estate in a fruit juice factory where they admitted that they did occasionally make up a white wine and herb drink for export. They, too, however, seemed to shrug off the subject and insisted that they had invented a much better drink which had raspberries in it! So I gave up. I suspect there once *had* been a tradition of something like a vermouth but it was swamped when the huge factories got going in the south of France and in Italy.

I went north from Chambéry around the bottom of the Lac du Bourget towards the Rhône. On the east bank I saw the lovely Roussette grape and on the west — like a little echo of Savoie — I found the wine region called Bugey. Previously unknown, it is now a celebrity wine in France thanks to being featured by a couple of Lyon's three-star restaurants as a local house wine. It is a reasonable idea really; after all the Rhône-side wines *below* Lyon knock out for exorbitant sums these days.

Monsieur Monin at Vognes can make superb wines and he can also talk the hind legs off a donkey. The wine was very good; in the end I favoured the Chardonnay from Monsieur Camille Crussy which was less demonstrative, less flamboyant and less expensive than some. It was a good clean wine and probably one of the cheapest Chardonnays in the world. There is another rarity in Bugey called Cerdon which I could not quite track down this time — better luck next time.

Maison Camille Crussy
Flaxieu 01350 Culoz

I continued back over the Rhône to Chautagne and discovered the very friendly co-op at Ruffieux. Monsieur Rosset is one of those super keen, young, bearded wine makers, fresh from college that one seems to find everywhere these days. He offered us several nice wines and a remarkable Pinot Noir which was really Burgundian in style with its toffee-ish full flavour and clean finish. Pinot Noir usually fails when grown anywhere outside Burgundy (unlike Cabernet Sauvignon which flourishes everywhere) so this is something worth pouncing on.

Monsieur Rosset
Cave Coopérative de Chautagne
73310 Ruffieux

A little further up the Rhône I came to Seyssel, which is a pretty town set among its vineyards on steep slopes east and west. It is around here that the Rhône valley narrows considerably up to Lake Geneva. I climbed laboriously up the eastern slope out of Seyssel, zig-zagging through vineyards until I had an almost aerial view of the town. Then I travelled

immaculately kept. The large rather fortress-like winery stood solemnly with stunning views over the lake.

Chateau de Ripaille, Thonon, Lake Geneva

along a picturesque road to Frangy passing through another steep valley also growing Roussette.

Maison Molex
Corbonnot 01420 Seyssel

I hit the autoroute a bit to the north and flew along towards Geneva, cheating slightly by only observing the vineyards of Bossey in the suburbs of Geneva at 140km/hr with foot firmly to the floor. On the map Ayze appeared to be just another sun-drenched slope, so I left the image undisturbed in my mind, as by now the fog was closing in. My careful circumnavigation of Switzerland (it is expensive you know) meant that I totally missed the vineyards of Ville-la-Grand. I was determined to make it to Crépy just because *everyone* has heard of Crépy — they even claim the Queen drinks it! Nonetheless, it turned out to be yet another speck on the oenological map. I found the estate of … the name eludes me but it is at Douvaine and virtually the only one worthy of the title 'estate'. The vineyards are splendid, and at 32 hectares the estate is really quite big and

Maison Mercier
Cave de Crépy
74140 Douvaine

Then, being nothing if not thorough, I went right along the N5, a lakeside drive, clocking off the Marin, Marignan and Ripaille vineyards. The first two are faint echoes of Crépy. Like Crépy they grow Chasselas which is what the Swiss grow over the other side of the lake and call Fendant (for which they charge the earth). You may remember that we also met some Chasselas way back in Pouilly-sur-Loire. Ripaille, on the other hand, is quite different. It is one of the most stunning castles I have ever seen standing, as it does, on its promontory at Thonon-les-Bains. Around its walls are immaculate vineyards, and the wine which it produces is a Vin de Pays and rather nice, but unfortunately sold almost exclusively on the gate for rather too much money. So, while nice to see, I decided to leave the buying to you when you pass on your holidays.

—STAGE 18—
Jura

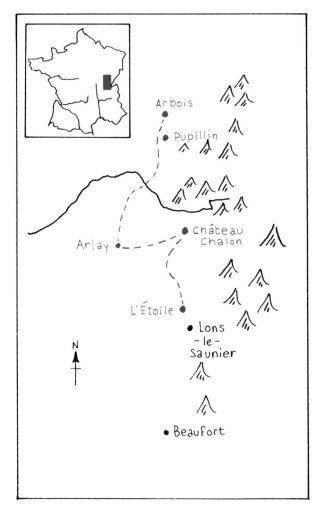

THE Jura remained the only sizeable wine region of France that I had never visited. I had driven through it a couple of times on the way back from Italy but never stopped to look around. I wonder why? Perhaps it was the name Henri Maire. Who? Henri Maire, the greatest living wine merchant in France. Henri Maire *is* the Jura. With about 340 hectares of vineyard, he must have the biggest holding in France by far and fittingly almost all the publicity is his too. I have marvelled for years how approximately every sixth house on every major road in France bears the ageing enamelled sign 'Vin Fou, Henri Maire'. For me the Jura just seemed to be a Maire solo, and hence I did not visit.

Back in about 1975, however, I did receive a case of wine from a small Jura producer. The dumpy bottles of old yellow wine began to give me a strong urge to visit the Jura. And here I am, a mere ten years later! I drove into Arbois around seven at night; Henri Maire was still selling wine in the little town which nestles comfily in the lee of the Jura hills. Along one of its new sleepy streets stands the riverside house of the first great wine scientist, one Louis Pasteur, who also did other works they tell me.

I stayed at the Hôtel de Paris which is easily the best place to learn about the Jura because the owner/chef, André Jeunet, knows the area 'comme sa poche'. The Côtes-du-Jura AOC is the largest appellation and covers about 60

villages throughout the area, most of which lie on the western flank of the attractive, rocky Jura hills. Arbois AOC is the second largest and covers the area surrounding the town of Arbois. Pupillin is a little village up the hill that obviously thinks that its wine is a touch better than the rest as it recently acquired its own appellation: Arbois-Pupillin AOC. These areas all make red, rosé and white wines as well as a little of the extraordinary 'vin jaune'. Château-Chalon AOC is a very small appellation which makes a minute amount of what is supposed to be the best vin jaune. Perhaps the least known appellation is l'Etoile AOC which is also tiny and makes both white and yellow. All this adds up to just over 1000 hectares, whereas at the height of its popularity the Jura had about twenty times that.

Returning, for a moment, to my sojourn in Arbois, I found a most attractive 'tasting shop' (a bit unprofessional, but in this case a worthwhile lapse). Madame Rolet, wife of the grower, with her small children about her skirts, introduced me to a very different kind of Jura white which I found irresistible. The normal white wines of the area are usually made from the Savignin grape but the Rolet family also grow Chardonnay. And their wine seemed to have made a move towards the vin jaune, that is to say it had acquired some 'flor'. Flor *(Saccharomyces bayanus)* is what makes 'fino' sherry; it also makes vin jaune. It is a kind of yeast which grows on the surface of certain wines as they lie in their barrels and forms a protective skin. This not only inhibits oxydization so that the wine stays fresh, but also allows it that unmistakable nutty-sherry flavour.

Etablissements Rolet Père et Fils
Montigny-les-Arsures
39600 Arbois

The Jura seems to be the only part of France where this flor chooses to live. Classic vins jaunes live for at least six years in little barrels with this flor working away at them and the evaporation concentrating them. It is perhaps not surprising, therefore, that they cost the earth. Monsieur Rolet's wine, however, is only a touch 'flor-ed' and consequently very interesting and much cheaper. One of the questions frequently asked by visitors to this region is 'What do you do with vin jaune?' I decided to try to find some answers and in doing so discovered that it went excellently with chicken; it would probably also be fine with veal, pork, duck and fish. As a rule of thumb, the extra flor flavour is best described as a nuttiness, so where nuts could conceivably be added to a dish, this wine is likely to harmonize.

There are a fair number of tasting shops in Arbois; in fact, a real hard-nosed, mean person could happily spend a day there as many of the emporiums offer free tastings. I eventually managed to drag myself away and on the outskirts of the town saw a sign to Pupillin. I could not resist the road leading up into the hills and I followed it round and round until I came to this little one street village. Absolutely everybody had a sign out selling their wine, so it was hard to choose. I saw a small cooperative and trundled in. A gentleman who must have been a wrestler in earlier days advanced upon me. He was as broad as he was long and I knew immediately that I would be buying wine here! The wine was, in fact, very good and just how good I only realized later when the Pupillin-Arbois wines beat the others in a blind tasting I organized back in England.

Fruitière Vinicole de Pupillin
Coopérative des Vignerons du Village
39600 Arbois

I also liked their light red (a more apt term in this case than rosé). It is amber-red coloured rather than pink and it is drunk in the manner of, say, a Beaujolais (that is, a light wine for lunches which comes out well either cold or room temperature). It is made from the Poulsard grape

which makes it fruity and low in tannin. Their white was good too. It was made purely from the Savignin grape which occurs nowhere else and is *not,* as many books say, related to the Traminer. It is a strong, almost beefy, dry white which is concentrated and keeps well (as I discovered by accident). The Arbois Blanc is one of the relatively few dry whites these days which repays a bit of ageing.

I drove further south to Arlay and met Monsieur Bourdy. Arlay is quite hard to find and Bourdy's place itself necessitates a certain amount of asking the way, until, literally, at the end of the track one arrives at a very comfy-looking farmhouse. The man who answered the door was Christian Bourdy who now runs the business. He is a big man as well as being very academic; I was immediately in awe. As he led me down a long, narrow, dark passage I had thoughts of old Badger and his house in *Wind in the Willows*. (My literary development obviously petered out around seven.) We all sat round the dining table in a dark room unchanged this century (antimacassars and aspidistras) and talked about how long it had taken me to get there. Monsieur Bourdy's impeccable filing system produced the original letter I wrote in 1975! I got the impression that Monsieur Bourdy writes a lot of letters. I suppose if Henri Maire is the great showman/champion of the Jura, then the Bourdy family are the up-market, intellectual champions who are always seeking to improve the region's renown through the writing of long, academic letters.

Cave Jean Bourdy
Arlay 39140 Bletterans

Christian is also a farmer, however, and that day he had just returned from pruning his half-hectare of Château-Chalon down the road. It was a bitter day, but the last thing a wise wine maker delegates is his pruning. As we talked, I saw through the window a well-wrapped up old man — Monsieur Jean Bourdy — walking slowly in the garden. Down in the cellars, Christian gave me a very thorough tasting and produced the most elegant red Jura wines I encountered on the trip. Apparently Arlay is particularly strong on reds as well as being unique in having more red vineyards than white (this dates back to the dukes of Burgundy who owned the Château d'Arlay at one stage and brought their drinking preferences with them).

I particularly liked the Etoile white which was thick, soft and aromatic with no hint of flor and totally dry. Afterwards, with considerable reverence, I was poured sips of the 'vin jaune de garde' or 'yellow wine for keeping'. This was a fruity, full and rich wine with a sherry nose exquisitely reminiscent of fruit cake — but for a price which makes it definitely only for special occasions. It is so fabulously concentrated (50 per cent of the wine evaporates in the six years before it is bottled) that it will keep for 100 years (provided the corks last). Christian is in the middle of re-corking his vast collection of ancient wines; sadly he declined my offer of help! You can, I suppose, drink this wine as a superior sort of sherry. I have just retasted a bottle I opened two months ago; I had kept it cold and it was impeccable, making me think of green walnuts,

Near Arlay.

Château-Chalon (most of it)

hazelnuts, almonds and candied fruit.

Then came the Château-Chalon AOC which was even greater — but heavens, the price. Christian explained that this wine is now rationed (which is a well-known crafty-French-wine-maker ploy). The appellation just covers 25 hectares and they only harvest five years in six; but add to this evaporation and a fair number of American, German and Japanese wine-freaks desperate for the stuff and it is clear why the price is going crazy. Besides, it is a good investment because they will never be able to make more of it than they do now.

Afterwards we went to see the Château-Chalon vineyards. Twenty-five hectares may be a modest single estate in other wine areas but here it is all there is. The reason they will not expand is because it is a unique sheltered and steep slope. Château-Chalon is not a single estate, there are many owners of tiny plots. The village itself is perched way up on a high cliff; it is a pretty but nevertheless 'working' village full of muck and tractors. From the belvédère I discovered a view down onto the unique vineyard below with its tiny plots, some cared for and some less so.

They usually harvest grapes for vin jaune in November when they are good and shrivelled. All jaunes are sold in the traditional *clavelin* bottle which is an odd shape and only holds 62cl. I would love to know how they got this past the EEC mandarins.

Lastly, I went to L'Etoile AOC to keep an appointment with a little cooperative. I arrived to be greeted by three chickens and bolted shutters.

Such is viticultural France. Thus I ended a foray into the Jura having managed to extract a few bottles of precious vin jaune but having given up on the Vin de Paille which is another speciality but much less remarkable, in my view. It is essentially a dessert wine made from grapes which are dried on straw mats before being fermented, hence the name *paille*.

After my tour around this unique and thriving wine region I cannot pretend that my discoveries are bargains. Really good Jura wines are not cheap; they are also a bit different, and perhaps meant for the adventurers among us.

The Clavelin

—STAGE 19—
Côte de Nuits

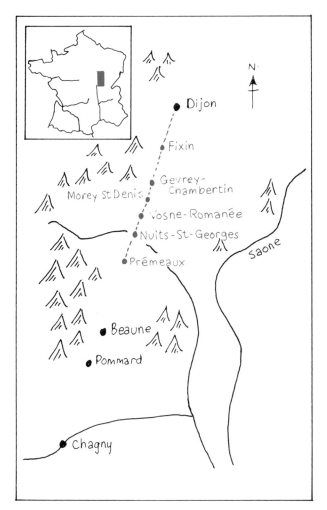

THERE is nowhere on the wine map more sacred and nowhere that you should approach with more caution than the Côte de Nuits — unless it is the Côte de Beaune. These two east-facing limestone escarpments are really as one (the separation is purely political) and the whole length of it from Dijon to Chagny is called the Côte d'Or. This narrow ribbon is the heart of Burgundy and, I imagine, the most expensive agricultural land in the world.

There is only one vineyard site where I regularly stop the car, get out and just stand looking at, and muddying my feet in, a bit of reddish earth — La Romanée-Conti; it is like a shrine. And I have not even tasted any Romanée-Conti! It is the most expensive wine in the world and theoretically the ultimate. I am frightened to taste the ultimate just yet. But caution is just as appropriate as reverence in an area where wines are so astonishingly valuable and in such short supply that there are always strong temptations to trickery.

My habit is to play safe by buying only estate-bottled wines, but this is not so easy in Burgundy. The fragmented nature of the vineyard holdings means that the big merchants are the only ones to give any large scale cohesion to the business. And although I accept that many merchants produce good, sound products, they always seem to me to lack the individuality that is the delight of this region, where the locals can spend hours discussing the relative merits of wines from neighbouring plots no bigger than the average back garden.

I visited the Machard de Gramont brothers who had moved to Prémeaux, just down the road from Nuits-St-Georges. Although only two brothers (Arnaud, who makes the wine and Bertrand, who generally oversees) are involved directly, there were, perhaps still are, two others. Whatever the case, everybody in Burgundy knows that it was the eldest brother's very rich wife who financed the de Gramont's estate expansion to what was, for Burgundy, a considerable size. They also know that the recent divorce deprived the de Gramonts of much finance and several fine *parcelles* of vineyards. The lady has since done a deal with an old négociant house who produces her wine, but it tastes different now that Arnaud's hand of genius is no longer in its making. Arnaud and Bertrand struggle on with a much smaller estate and new cellars.

Domaines Machard de Gramont
rue Gassendi
21700 Nuits-St-Georges

A man under a tractor — nothing serious, I think — at last directed me to the new Machard de Gramont cellars. Unfortunately, the road was up, it was pitch dark and raining 'pikes' (as my old French master claimed they said), but I got there. Bertrand shepherded me around what I think was a vast stone farm building (it was very dark and could have been a prison). I noticed with relief that they had managed to hold on to their extraordinary collection of old wooden fermenting tubs of all shapes and sizes. They are vital to a Burgundian estate (a laughable expression really as even the grandest resembles just a jumble of allotments spread over a dozen villages).

These are, if I decipher my notes correctly, the Machard de Gramont brothers' holdings:

At Chambolle Musigny	3 ares
At Nuits-St-Georges:	
Les Damodes (simple)	12 ares
Les Damodes (1er cru)	14 ares
Pierrier Noblot	10 ares
Les Hauts Pruliers	10 ares
Les Valrous (1er cru)	14 ares
Les Haut Poirets	8 ares
other	18 ares
At Aloxe Corton:	
Les Morets	12 ares
At Savigny-Les-Beaune:	
Les Guettes (1er cru)	15 ares
other	10 ares
At Beaune:	
Les Epenots	5 ares

DeGramont.

At Pommard:

Clos Blanc (1er cru)	13 ares
Les Vaumurians	2 ares

At Puligny:

Les Houilleres	20 ares

(An are is one hundredth of a hectare, about one fiftieth of an acre.)

My question is, how on earth do you vinify that lot, taking care to preserve particular characteristics of the bouquet and of each individual site? The answer, in many estates, is 'quite miraculously', especially since they only have a row of big 100 hecto vats. Perhaps the Volnay 'Des Reynards', or whatever, just somehow stays naturally separated from the Pommard 'Petites Vierges' during the fermentation and can be drawn off separately? God probably does like Burgundy, but I prefer to believe in Arnaud's odd-sized tubs.

A very long, steep flight of stairs leads to some vast cellars of some grandiosity. The fine gothic arches are marred, sadly, by the sheets of polythene which seem to infect cellar doorways throughout Burgundy after a cold harvest as an essential accompaniment to the electric radiators and fan heaters. They are desperate to keep their barrels above about 20°C so the newly fermented wine will 'do its malo' (secondary fermentation) at this point rather than at some later date when it might frighten the customers.

When it came to tasting, we completed the list and that meant four rows of about twenty barrels each from every 'climat'. We were like a scrum of five, moving from barrel to barrel like doctors doing their ward rounds. The process went: bang of the hammer either side of the bung, sideways clout, out it comes, in goes glass syphon, pause, apply thumb for vacuum and remove a sparkling shaft of ruby. Then follows the swirl, peer, sniff, gargle, eyes raised heavenward, long pause and finally the discreet ping into the corner.

The dreaded struggle to write down something which is both clever and accurate comes next. I know people who can and do write half a page on every wine systematically, taking into account colour, weight, length, aroma, bouquet and aftertaste. I, like the ex-President, cannot walk and chew wine at the same time. Instead I taste, stand there and hope some bolt of blinding inspiration will hit. No bolt, no words, it is as simple as that. The way I see it is that as I must gargle around 4,000 wines a year and if I try to write notes on that lot and then wade through to find a buy, I will never get home again. It is a crude but effective filter system; unless I get very excited and the inspiration comes on strong, I go no further. Thus it was that dark, wet, November night in Prémeaux when I marked my card. The trouble is that when I come back at Easter it is quite likely all will have changed!

We turned to the cellar where the 1983s lurked and, 'Mon Dieu', were they monsters. Being kept at 14°C is really nothing, but the heat of the wine had my two fellow travellers and trainee tasters reeling. (That will teach them not to be so greedy and not to swallow it next time!) Another Annus Mirabilis is coming along here, no doubt, and Hugh Johnson will have to hunt around for more asterisks. Alas, this probably means that lots of it will be bought for quite the wrong reasons and dished out too young. Anyway, I am going to lock mine up in a cave and forget about it.

At Vosne-Romanée I pulled just off the main road at an undistinguished bungalow, to be greeted by a loud dog. Monsieur Pernin took us down some steps by the side of his bungalow into his plain, small cellar. Here we found built-in concrete vats, some old *pièces*, piles of cobwebby bottles, firewood and an impressive collection of plaques and medal certificates on the wall. I also noticed a shelf of bottled fruit and vegetables and realized that I was in the private den of a private man; it was the sort of place where some of us are happiest just pottering. But this is a stone's throw from La Romanée-Conti, and these bottles are worth a fortune. So although I did get vertigo at the prices, I do not now regret my purchases and now that I am adjusted for inflation, I do not regret a drop.

Domaine Pernin-Rossin
Vosne-Romanée

I travelled on past Vougeot and Morey to Gevrey and the boy wine maker, Bernard Bachelet, who looks about 14 (but then quite a lot of policemen do, too, these days which, I gather, happens as one gets older). He lives right on the N74 at Gevrey and he, too, has a plastic-hung cellar. He has another cellar up in the old village which is entered by a near vertical shaft quite unsuited to fat, middle-aged British merchants. I made for the pile of bottles standing proud in the middle of the cellar and came upon a 1982 Les Corbeaux 1er Cru Chambertin with a heavenly bouquet.

Domaine Bernard Bachelet
Gevrey-Chambertin

I pressed on to Fixin, and the run-down château with the mad monk. Well Philippe Joliet is no monk really and totally sane, but let me describe the scenario. The Château La Perrière was once a home for the dukes of Burgundy, so it

Bachelet's Cellar

is a real château which is rarer than rare here. It is also dilapidated, although part of the dilapidation has been caused by the builders who are trying to 'de-dilapidate' it. I ambled through a small gothic doorway in a side turret and down a circular stairway to what must have once been a chapel. It was vast, ill lit and cobwebby and held a monstrous old wine press and some huge old casks. One light bulb in an alcove threw into stark relief a bearded, hunched, dishevelled person dressed in a robe and bent over a bubbling flask. The blue flame, the stare and absence of response to my nervous 'good afternoon' made for an awkward moment. Then somehow a thaw set in; the silence was shyness rather than anger and the robe proved to be an over large sweater. The alembic was just for testing pH levels and soon the apparition opened a bottle of wine and a little later we were all great friends.

Philippe Joliet
Fixin

By this stage I had more or less run the length of the Côte de Nuits, although here, more than anywhere else it was difficult to be thorough. It is not just that every village has its own appellation but all the individual Premier and Grand Cru sites have their own appellations also. That means that there are well over 150 appellations in the space of just one average Bordeaux appellation. As much as I would have liked to have stayed to drink my way through the lot, I could not. Many of the vineyards along the Côte are not considered good enough for Cru status or even to carry their village's name. They generally end up as just Côte de Nuits. More interesting are the Hautes Côtes de Nuits which come from the slopes behind the first slope. Not benefiting from the same balmy climate as the Côte itself, they tend to make a rather tart wine. But the 1983 vintage, thanks to the very hot summer, produced a good, soft wine. Claude Cornu's 1983 is a beauty. He is the umpteenth generation wine-maker at Magny-les-Villers which cannot be much more than half a mile from the great hill of Corton (even if it is half a mile in the wrong direction). The wine is a lovely, fruit-filled Burgundy and excellent value.

Domaine Claude Cornu
Magny-les-Villers

—STAGE 20—
Alsace-Lorraine

I ALWAYS like to enter Alsace via the Bonhomme pass. It is more dramatic and scenic than going in round either end of the Vosges mountains. It also drops you right down upon Kaysersberg which is my favourite Alsace village. Alsace is a narrow strip of land squeezed between the Vosges and the Rhine. The vineyards are an *extremely* narrow strip squeezed between the mountain pines and the valley cabbage fields (for this is the home of *choucroute*).

It was snowing heavily as I approached across dreary Lorraine, so there was the added thrill — with badly worn tyre treads — of 'would I make it?' I did, albeit very slowly. Winding down round and round through all those dark pines, I saw happy skiers pass us, it must have been the first decent fall for them that year. I continued down through the upland villages and pastures past Monsieur Miclo's little distillery. (He has another on Tahiti and a range of white alcohols that runs from bilberry, cherry and William pear to mango, pineapple and passion fruit!)

Soon the Kaysersberg castle loomed up in the dusk on the left and I drove right into a Christmas card. The narrow cobbled streets, the overhanging, timberframed houses with steep snow-covered roofs, the bright shop windows and the frozen fountain made a magical scene. Alsace

is the only wine region I actually prefer to visit in the winter.

Only a few hundred yards down the valley is the next village, Kientzheim. It is smaller but just as pretty. Between the two is the most celebrated vineyard in all Alsace, the steep, granite

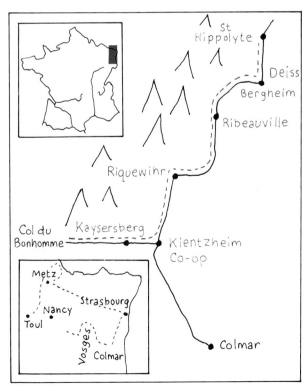

Typical wine-maker's sign in the Alsace region.

123

Schlossberg. The snow was quite deep now but I pushed through to the Coopérative Vinicole knowing that a welcome awaited. Monsieur Hauss has still not retired, he has probably forgotten to. He is very much the absent-minded professor type and very, very clever. The place runs like clockwork because, I like to think, he got all that sorted out 30 years ago when he founded the place and now he just amuses himself by pottering round his vats and his halls of bottles. His No.2, the long-suffering Petitdemange, really looks after the operation.

Monsieur Hauss or Monsieur Petitdemange
Cave Vinicole de Kientzheim Kaysersberg
Kientzheim
68240 Kaysersberg

I spent all too few welcome seconds in the warm office before being dragged off to taste every vat in the immaculate cellar. Of course, in Alsace there is a lot to taste because they do not just make one or two styles per cellar but six at least and usually many more. They are varietal mad here in contrast to the rest of France which is site mad. Here, they have always concentrated on the individual grape varieties, which are all widely different yet all come under the one overall geographic appellation of Alsace. The rest of France, of course, tends to play down what it is made of and concentrate on just which particular vineyard or village it was grown in. Unfortunately, in Alsace today they have now decided to do both, so now it is getting really complicated. The best vineyard sites — Schlossberg was the first — are being carefully plotted and identified as Grand Cru sites.

The tastings generally turn out to be long affairs. Unusually, on this occasion, we started with the big 'hit' of the visit, from the 'doing business' angle. The current vintage was excessively copious, but not as concentrated and generally wonderful as its immediate predecessor. But one of the four vats of Pinot Blanc we tried was like the puppy in the pet shop window... irresistible. The cold-numbed fingers continued to write notes through the Rieslings and they came out something like this: 'pure steel rails; very much a with food wine; not aperitif.' The Muscats were described as 'greener than usual'.

Kaysersberg

Alsace.

We moved on to the Tokays (or Pinot Gris if you prefer) before ending, as always, on the big blowsy Gewürztraminers. POW!

There was a nasty moment when it looked rather as if the Hauss's enthusiasm was going to drag us outside into the blizzard where in the stainless steel *batterie* more wines were rapidly turning into giant ice-lollies (it does them good, believe it or not). I did not fancy the same fate and fortunately Petitdemange diplomatically intervened and suggested postponing the bottle tasting till the morning and going off to dinner. His sister and her husband run a simple but ever-so-warm little hostelry up in the hills at Lapoutroie. Our spirits rose at the sight of the blazing fire, but Monsieur Hauss thought we should look round Monsieur Baldinger's cellar first. So it was a case of coats back on chaps (but with a nice glass of Alsace Crémant and a few warm little onion tartlets, the tour was not so bad). Crémant (Alsace wine champenized) is a booming new fashion rather than an old tradition. Monsieur Hauss is very proud of his own Crémant but just wishes the locals would refrain

from adding Cassis to it. (Personally, I think the locals are right.) Traditionally it is the region's Tokays and Gewürztraminers that are drunk as aperitifs.

Dinner was, among other things, a trout 'au Riesling' fresh from the cage in the stream right by the kitchen door, and a Munster mega-smelly cheese which I was taught to eat with a pinch of cumin seed. On one very early visit here in my old van Monsieur Hauss would insist that I take home what he termed 'a really good' Munster. He squeezed every one in the shop till he found one that squeezed right back. Before I had gone a mile I had to take the thing out of the cab and put it in the back with the wine. At Southampton the customs officer got awkward and wanted a full turn-out. He was going to count every bottle which meant that I would be there all day. He stood there all beady-eyed and suspicious and much too close. As the tailgate shot up he got hit by a wall of over-ripe Munster aroma. It was a warm day. Vainly flapping my declaration documents before his nose he did the fastest count of one hundred cartons I have ever seen and left at a run. I cleared within minutes.

The Hostellerie de l'Abbaye d'Alspach is one of my favourite hotels in all France. It is very cheap and run by a young couple part-time. The Schwartzs are phenomenally hard-working like most of Alsace. It is only six rooms or so and lies tucked away down a back alley complete with cobbled yard and one of those old covered balcony-bridges. There was nobody there when I arrived, just a note 'Your keys are in the doors'. Informal, but well heated and in the morning the *caveau/wein-stub* restaurant was in full swing long before I was. Do they ever sleep?

After breakfast I went to take photographs of the enchanting snow covered vines and rooftops. Up the vigneron tracks and into the Schlossberg it was sheer madness with the car going every direction at once. Back at the cooperative I tried the full range of massive 1983s, some 1982s and a valedictory 1971 Gewürztraminer from the Kaefferkopf vineyard for which my notes say 'taste of...' and end speechless. I think this was the first wine I ever bought here, I certainly wish I had been able to keep a few bottles!

Monsieur Hauss's tasting room has a vast mural showing a view of Kientzheim and Kaysersberg bemoated and walled in medieval times; it also depicts the nearby Ammerschwihr

and Sigolsheim. Knights on horseback suggesting inter-village and inter-lordling warfare complete the picture. Still today some villages are Catholic and some Protestant and the rivalry is non-violent but intense. Kientzheim has a town gateway in the form of a huge gargoyle face which is said to be (and clearly is) sticking its tongue out at Sigolsheim! Kientzheimers refer to Sigolsheimers as 'sausage-beaters' which is very rude (I cannot cope with the dialect which is like a particularly incomprehensible German). Sigolsheimers refer to Kaysersbergers (surely excluding their most famous son, Albert Schweitzer) as 'sloe-bellies'. That could be very useful information to you when you visit. I staggered off to one more cellar before lunch.

I deal or have dealt with several family estates in Alsace, but the Deiss family in Bergheim are my favourites of the moment. They are a very family affair: Marcel Deiss (great grandfather) is deceased but lives on as a registered name; Deiss (grandfather) still works a hard day in the vineyards while Jean-Michel Deiss does wonderful things as cellar master. He, one gets the impression, is the motor that drives the concern; he always has new ideas and talks off the proverbial hind legs. He is an engineer wine maker and has built this extraordinary mantis-like tractor that looks more suited to Cape Canaveral, Santa Pod or the King's Road. It has got four motors and its wheelbase expands, contracts or tilts depending on the terrain.

Marcel Deiss et Fils
15 Route du Vin
68750 Bergheim

Here I indulged in another mammoth tasting

round the vats. Jean-Michel has split all his wines by vineyard as well as grape variety, so I tried several versions of all the types tried at Kientzheim plus a Sylvaner — lightest of whites — and Pinot Noir — the red of Alsace. (In the Middle Ages Alsace grew mostly red in fact.) I particularly liked his Muscat, Tokay and Gewürz, I think!

We had a big lunch (with lots of wines) and then had the bottle tasting. By about five I was punch drunk on flavours (but not alcohol as I had dutifully spat away all day — except at lunch, people generally do not like that). My last notes read 'Riesling is a vertical wine, Gewürztraminer is a horizontal wine'! Now what do *you* make of that? When we left, my plans to show my travelling companions a bit of Riquewihr and Eguisheim — more ravishing villages — went by the board. It was all I could do to get us to the first hotel on the outskirts of Strasbourg.

The following day I investigated the somewhat uncertain references to Lorraine vineyards that one sees on some maps: Vins de Moselle. 'Moselle' is the French name for the German 'Mosel' and British wine drinkers are oddly confused about this.

At Metz, pollution seems to dominate. Power cables, pylons, factories and general wasteland rule. And to think that the oily stuff down there which gurgles through the swamp is the Moselle, perhaps the most picturesque wine river in Europe. It certainly has a bad patch around Metz! But I turned north towards the German border and just before I reached it, the river became more Mosel-like and dipped into a deep, winding valley … and there were the vineyards, French Moselle wines do exist. Or do they? Chatting to growers I encountered a certain evasiveness and a few surprises. It turns out that most of the vineyards are cultivated by Germans who take their grapes over the border back home. As far as the French authorities are concerned there is no appellation here, no VDQS and no Vin de Pays. The bottles of the Coteaux de Contz I got hold of may or may not have been Pinot Noir for the labels were, technically, quite illegal! Had the wine been good that would not have bothered me, but it was not!

I had not yet finished with the Moselle and travelled back south past Metz again. Another relic area is the Côtes de Toul VDQS which actually does exist. I had been through it once before and I also knew that wines from there had won prizes in Paris. Armed with a list of the prizewinners, I searched. In the nick of time, just before lunch, I turned up at Monsieur Pierre Lang's workshop. This is the furniture-making heartland of France and Monsieur Lang is knocking out a nice little grandfather clock. Bemused by my interest in wine rather than wood, he nonetheless quickly changed hats and took us to his *bougerie*. This is not quite so worrying as it sounds; it refers to one of the local traditions of above-ground cellars full of odd-looking upright barrels of Gamay, or at least the local style of Gamay. It is decidedly unusual being grey … not pink, but grey. It is also very acid when it is young and subsequently mellows, as acid wines often do, most mellifluously. If, like me, you like to try weird wines occasionally, this is one for you.

Monsieur Pierre Lang
Côtes de Toul
rue de Charmes
54170 Mont le Vignoble